The 7 secrets of intelligence

| Daniel Ferdinand Von Rodericksson

This book is a work of nonfiction. While every effort has been made to ensure the accuracy and completeness of the information contained herein, the author and publisher assume no responsibility for errors, inaccuracies, omissions, or any consequences arising from the use of the information in this book. The views expressed are those of the author and do not necessarily reflect the opinions or policies of the publisher.

PREFACE

Intelligence is one of the most adored qualities a human being can possess, very few people have been described as being exceptionally intelligent, they are automatically brought into fame and so many other purposes for which it can be used. Even so, even these people were not exempt from the circumstances of life, and their mere talent was not enough, they had a set of secrets, habits, that have allowed them to utilize the full potential of their minds. In this book I offer the reader tips, or habits, that everyone can apply, and that can lead you towards a higher degree of intelligence. These habits, unlike the habits of the common person, open the mind of the person to higher degrees of intellect, and the person himself will be amazed at the degree of intellect they can reach, even if they only apply a little of these tips. The sole object, after reading so many books about intelligence or books that have spoken about the same, after understanding the lives of geniuses, and people in general that are intelligent, I have seen them all being driven by a few common denominators that make them stand out from the rest. Not only that, I have seen these great truths being manifested in my own persona. I have seen how these little changes can have great effects, and to what extent intelligence is simply a matter of habits, I bring these certain "secret" habits to you, so that you can also apply them. Intelligent peoples have all this in common, that they have passed down these habits or customs embedded in their culture from generation to generation. Intelligence, I seek to prove through a set of chapters that aim to employ the practicality of the tips, can be at the hands of all, intelligence is not a secret or quality that only a few are given or gifted, anyone can ever improve their intelligence by these secrets, intelligence comes in many presentations, and a little of this can bring much of that, and a few changes can have an everlasting and powerful many effects in your life and potential. Everyone or many have the potential to enter this state of genius, for being a genius, I will now explain, is not a special quality of the person, but of the mind, it is a state of mind, and a state of mind that can be achieved by anyone, just like any emotion that a person would feel or a state of focus a person has, intelligence also works that way. Intelligence, with these tips, can be used for the right and righteous things, it can be fertilized to help humanity and expand the frontiers of knowledge and benevolence. Intelligence can, if learned and constituted in the right form, change the world and turn humanity towards the right path, and that I write this book for.

"An intelligent person is never afraid or ashamed to find errors in his understanding of things." — Bryant H. McGill

Introduction to intelligence and the application of secrets to the same

Intelligence has existed as a paradigm of human society since a long time ago, for instance, back in the days of the ancient empires and civilizations, it is obvious to assume, and this we may do at any hypothetical time or epoch, that those who had a high degree of intelligence were valued in society, and that the more this intelligence had a substantial application in this society the higher the respect this person earned or was merited by society. Intelligent people had the mission to ease the lives of others, to do that hard mental work that many, they thought to themselves, were unable to execute.

 As human society progresses in countless ways, so do our countless the many intelligences that exist in human society, and the many people that adapted themselves to them. In cultures as that of the Jews or the Japanese, intelligence is extremely important in society, especially in its sense of application or profession. Intelligence is an interaction of the individual with the collective, nothing more complex.

The unit tries to understand the field which it inhibits, it tries to become one with all aspects within it, for example, if the sun moves a certain way, if the moon rotates a certain manner, the individual will try to understand it. If the villager sees the water flowing through the river, or the singing of the birds, he will try to better understand the reason why all these things occur. Intelligence is the understanding of patterns in the All for the survival of the self.

Intelligence is another phase of evolution, but that a being may be intelligent does not mean superior. In fact, one of the greatest problems of human society is that this intelligence, through the aberrant will of the human, is used for negative purposes and understood from a wrong perspective. How many could have achieved their true intelligence before if they were not guided by this sense of truth and ego. For this reason, intelligent or not, it is really hard to decipher the potential of a person for such, for it may not always be expressed in its optimal form.

The intelligent may have, at many times, utilized this power for the wrong pursuits, they have tried to enslave the people with ideas, they knew, would only benefit them, but not the other. Intelligence may be used for evil or for good. When it is used for evil, we see that intelligence cannot go very far, and that no one can achieve their true potential, but when intelligence is based upon benevolence, we can see it achieve its greatest form. Intelligence can only really succeed, as it is shown in this book, when it is used for the good of others, when it is used for the advancement of the righteous morals and codes, and not for the selfish advancement of the few-selves.

 Our intellectuality has been going through a process of stagnation of society because people did want to let go of the control they had on the people. They wanted these dogmas to be maintained, for they know that through them people can be enslaved and they cannot reach their true potential, and there is nothing worse for the intellect, for the advancement of a society than them.

The first step, then, is to be free from any sort of limitation or dogma, to be free from that which you previously thought was a different way, for I tell you had you not done so, none of these principal would be applicable, for they occur only on the mind free from limitation, fear, and so many other embarks the mind take, and that lead to all kinds of things except that root or seed that would open the world around these principles I am about to tell you. You cannot be closed, the first requirement is that you must be open, you must be tolerant, and you must work for the best good of others. You must not seek for yourself. The greatest empires in history have fallen because of this one reason.

The state of society always starts in our own hearts. If you desire to become your best self, you cannot close yourself to these ideas, or to any idea at all. You must always learn and work for yourself so that you are able to learn, and properly develop your intelligence. So you must not develop your understanding of the other by the others, for by doing so you already admit that you have become a slave to the collective, think in such terms, and be guided solely by your own intellect.

It is when our outside becomes more important than our inside, that the letter is destroyed and suppressed. Different people are born with different intellectual capacities, different personalities and different strengths in their characters and mental strength that allow them to express these, they are also born in different circumstances. Having a combination of all these is key to developing your intelligence in the right manner, you must have a set of traits beyond the secrets I'm about to present in order that these secrets may work the way they must work. These secrets are not special to intelligence, but they mostly work for any of these other traits, or for that matter, for anything you want to achieve in life.

If you follow these tips, intelligence will easily and naturally knock at your door, and the secrets will, even without me telling you, display themselves at your door, but if you don't, you may not even apply these secrets even if I'm already telling them to you. Many have tried to unveil what you are about to listen to but they were fortunate enough, but so you are... listen carefully..

Part 1: The Secrets of Intelligence

"Nature is the source of all true knowledge." - Leonardo da Vinci

1. The Secrets of Natural Affinity

In nature, in all that it encompasses, even to the deepest miles of the sea, and to the highest ends of the cosmos visible in our starry night, there are certain patterns that must be fulfilled. These patterns are based upon one primordial law in the All, that is, the Law of Balance. Everything must be balanced to work, even the truth in itself, the application of the same, is all based upon the factor of balance. Our body functions according to balance, and disease is the result of imbalance.

 All machines must work under certain laws which ultimately are of balance. Our ecosystem also works according to balance and certain forces within the All, nothing can work outside this law of balance. Life is balance and balance is life, and whenever this balance is no longer, there cannot be more life, or life must translate itself into another form. Our minds are nothing but a mirroring of this universal mind that is bringing logic and balance into all things.

If our minds are alienated with this universal balance, they are aligned with universal intelligence, and thereafter, we may become perfect like nature itself. What is an airship? It is an imitation of the way in which waves fly. What is a car? It is an imitation of a large animal or a large rolling animal. What is the internet, what is the computer? It is an imitation of our brain, or an animal's brain. What is fire? Henceforth, we can go one by one through each invention and you would realize that their origin is a natural one.

When we look into the many arts and sciences that have come to fill the cases of libraries, we see a common pattern, that they all seek to imitate nature, and to understand it through the same. Even famous intellectual figures, like the Italian mathematician Fibonacci, discerned the mathematical patterns by understanding nature.

Leonardo Da Vinci created the helicopter by understanding birds, and machinated hidden numerical clues that reference nature. Isaac Newton discovered the laws of motion and gravity, too, by contemplating and afterwards, having the realization after the fall of that famous apple. Santiago and Cajal understood the human neurological system by understanding the branches of trees and landscapes. The examples are unlimited.

 Nature may not apparently have any number showing up, nature is only the theater and the many beings therein inhabiting are nothing but the actors, while the director, who knows it all, is ever hiding itself. The director will not reveal itself except through art. The director is not a showman, that's why he is invisible. The credit of finding all these patterns, like a labyrinth or puzzle, must be for those who are ignorant, and that is precisely the point of the game.

You may think that this alienation is already inside our brains, for our brains or minds, are too, a manifestation of nature. You are right. But, to see nature inside ourselves, is the point of the spiritual world, and in reference to the intellectual world, we must see nature outside. Even our brains, it is said, or our bodies, are not really us, but are only the scheme of nature working for our spirit. Thus, studying our brains, and all our corporeal functions, is too, the study of nature external to us. When we don't align with nature, one way or the other, we suffer much.

The process may be distinct to intellectuality in itself, but they are still, a reflection of the same principle. When you wake up in the morning, you must always do what you have to do to begin your day, and if you don't align, the rest of the will go down hill. If you don't adhere to certain principles, your body will get sick. If you don't sleep according to night and day, you will also get sleep deprivation and become fatigued. These are plain habits of health, but they are also a reflection of natural affinity. We don't align with nature when our will becomes aberrant and we oppose.

Therefore, those acts of so-called sin, evil, or any of such are also the correspondence of the opposition to this natural affinity. While people align with nature through their intellect, they are misaligned in so many other ways they do not become aware of. Affinity must be all round, affinity must not be one one type and then to neglect the other, for in the ultimate run, we are neglecting the overall factors of intelligence that are not merely those of the intellect. When we learn about nature, we may not enter such a natural state ourselves, for every part of our brain and minds must become tuned with it, so that these states of higher intelligence become innate in us. When the mind is one way aligned with those but not in others, this intelligence will suffer one way or the other.

To learn and acquire the intelligence of nature, is not solely a learning process but a transformational one. Such transformation must take place until our subconscious and our deepest intellectual abilities and storage become aligned with nature. When we become fully aligned with nature, all that is behind nature will be naturally revealed unto us. When we only align one part, all these parts of nature in correspondence from the unit to the macrocosmic will become compartmentalized in our subjective minds. The total intellectual affinity becomes available when every part of our thoughts and mental states, beliefs and emotions become aligned with nature and the law of balance. If such is not the case, intelligence will be retarted one way or the other.

 Everything we do must be natural, one way or the other, and even in the so-called irrationality, when there is naturality, there may also be rationality when it is revealed through intuition. Reason is not the sole cause of intelligence, or ability derived from the same, but there is intuition too ankled even in this reason, while the latter is at many times ignored by the philosophers. Nature develops, generates and degenerates through this intuition, through an irrational self-enveloped thinking. There is no Creator but Creation creates itself through intuition. We can become one and align with it to understand how it works, and our very self can understand the deepest aspects of the same. When we become aligned in intellect with our own nature, we become aligned with the deepest forces of the Cosmos.

Cosmos and self are the same, intelligence is deeply embedded in this ability to become one with all things, for there is no better way of understanding than through being and through consciousness. When we understand, there is no better way than to do it through the amplification of perfection. To align with all things is to become one with them, to be conscious of them, to perceive in so many different modes. This is how nature works. You may think that nature lacks intelligence, but this is only because you do not see it. No one is more intelligent than nature, and less so in so many modes and expressions as so does nature.

Nature is so powerful that it only has a way out, and a way in, meaning; it always renews itself, it will never stop existing, but it will always be changing into so many different forms. To become nature is to become the eternal changing moderation. There are always key principles attached to the laws of balance, but the elements following this balance always change. There is no regret, longing or melancholy for nature, for she knows that death does not exist, she knows all is change and relativism. This relativism is a key principle of intelligence, the principle of Adaptation. When we align with nature, we align with all that nature does to express itself, and the so many rules found therein, all these rules come under so many names, but they are all linked to our affinity with nature, or the means by which we change nature, in a natural way, to align with us.

All these secrets you know, have been quoted so many times, these laws have been known to the wise since ancient times, and they are all the expression of nature. The problem is that these laws may become too complicated to be practiced day to day. That's why I use the term, affinity with nature, for nature is closer to us than these laws, nature reveals all these laws to us in the easiest form, we just need to listen to her songs and contemplate her beauty. The problem is that humanity is lost in her own "beauty" and she ignores the beauty that is above all, that always works, and thus, provides intelligence. Human beauty, derived from their aberrant nature, is wasted at all times and brings evil and retardation, while natural beauty only brings intelligence and practicality.

Natural beauty can reveal all that which we never thought we could have knowledge of, understanding the silence of nature and the keys to the forbidden knowledge will be revealed without even having to move from your home. You do not need new books, or hidden knowledge to align with nature, ignore all these things made by imperfect humans, and change it for the perfect intelligence found within the natural books, that are hidden in every event and incident of nature. When all our factors and senses become one with nature, even knowledge is not needed, for the rules of one aspect become evident in them all, and this little curiosity for nature brings much that is impossible if it was otherwise used in other less natural aspects.

"Sex energy is the creative energy of all geniuses. There never has been, and never will be a great leader, builder or artist lacking in the driving force of sex."
— Napoleon Hill

---

2. The Secrets of Sexual Transmutation

When you think about sex, what do you notice, that your creativity is destroyed, you are destroyed, you cannot control yourself, you cannot take control of your higher qualities on the intellectual side. The control over your sexual instincts is of fundamental importance for your intellect. The ways in which this force affects intellectual capacity are multi-channeled. First, it affects the sexual force through the power of the neurotransmitters that are affected by its addictive power.

These neurotransmitters are a vital aspect of intelligence, and when the sexual force is not controlled they are severely affected. Another way in which the sexual force destroys intellect when not properly used is when the semen ways the lymph that should be used for intellectual power, this lymph works as a compliment to blood in the brain, as it does to any other part of the body, and so when lymph is not flowing through the brain in the right quantities, the brain will not work at its full potential.

The waste of lymph through semen itself also hurts the body in so many other ways that affect the cognitive function, and it drains nutrients and metabolic energy for the body, meaning; that the body has to use more energy than it should for it to work properly on the sexual function, and other functions of the body are affected, including, thereafter in conjunctive measurement, that of the brain and its psychic counterpart, called, the intellect.

On this last channel by which the sexual force is manifested, we see the following. That the sexual process, that of mating, be it in whatever of its forms, takes a large amount of psychic energy and resources. From a young age, and after that period called of the prepubescent, large amounts of such energies are wasted on this process of mating, especially on the psychic level.

We think way too long about and imagine how this process would be, so much so that most people, if not having the proper education about such a topic, end up becoming addicts, and sex becomes the greatest part of their lives. When we see animals, we see them not thinking all day long and all year long about the sexual mating process, but only during certain stations of the year, and even of their life. On the other hand, human beings think way too much about it, all year long and wherever so the hormones and any other psychic process determine it, without any clear restraint.

This energy, that animals, thanks to their instinct use properly, shall be used towards the process of procreating and creating the next generation, nothing else. The problem of human beings, is that this same intellect is the drawback that leads them towards a malfunction in the psychic propensities of the sexual kind, making them, because of their free-will, not moderate such mating process, but open it in such and so many ways, and different forms that it is completely distorted and aberrant. Through technology, their intellectual abilities, and much more, humanity has malformed this process into an unrecognizable waste of time and energy.

This creates a vicious cycle in which not only does sexual energy destroy the intellect, but this same channel, given its complexity and capacity of external ramification, over-rules into a regressive process, in which the sexual energy is wasted in so many forms except that which is necessary. This intellect and this highly emotional nature, given the mammalian nature of the human being, drives him towards romance, platonism, and so many other wastes of energy that are part of this same intellect.

The understanding of reality is completely undermined by such romantic, sexual and otherwise fetish and philia-like processes, some are natural, other are artificial and the product of the same lack of satisfaction by the same, given its poor transmutation towards the spiritual cause, as we shall explain shortly. When the mind is constantly seeking such sexual contentment, the human being is completely separated from reality, and their nature is not fulfilled.

The animal cannot ever think all day long, for it lives in nature and it must survive, all their cognitive abilities must be directed towards the natural aspect of their own existence and maintenance of the same. But human beings, given their own intellectual condition, have the chance to create such artificial environments in such processes that are relatively possible, and even absolutely possible, to such an extent that they lead to death. This death, that for the majority of cases takes form even before it actually occurs, happens in many forms. There is a process in yoga, a part of this science, called *brahmacharya*, meaning, to occupy your mind in Braham.

Now, this is at many times related to sexual energy, but in reality it refers to the occupation of the mind in God, the Creator, or Brahma, at all times, or for the right amount of time for that human mission to be effectively built. Now, when the human being is not only not focused on Brahma, but not focused on the Creation of Brahma, the human being will lose its nature, the nature not of the spiritual but of the intellectual way. This is because of the inherent nature of such a process, a crude one, one that leads to the lower instincts, and by such effect, the mind does not exercise to the proper force, the mind is ever or mostly latent on an activity that does not meet its standards to fulfill the right intellectual capacity.

The creative power of sexual energy is dumbfounded by that of its waste in an immoderate manner. It is said in the Bible that we are built on God's image, and if such is the case, in such microcosmic reflective *ultranza*, we are then endowed with many capacities of God, one of which is that of creating.

 Everyone has the capacity to imagine and create since we are children, but have we noticed, that the more we are indulgent in our sexual tendencies we get closer to adolescence, the more we suppress our imagination, and thereafter the innocence of the child is lost. Therefore, the loss of innocence by defect of the sexual contingencies is also the waste of the imaginative and creative power, and not only that, but the power to see the many creative patterns in the imagination of our father, for us and Him are one, in the one. To occupy so much energy in this process, destroys this creative power, especially in its most abstract portion.

Visualization is corrupted, for the more the addiction and animalism, the lesser our capacity to visualize, to see things as they are, and to transmute their forms into many different points of view over which a new perspective may be obtained. Therefore, the mind is accustomed to the simple, to the lower instinct, and thus it dies when not worked out, just like the muscle must be kept under strain so that it can keep growing and developing. When we think and memorize, this process is greatly difficult and the energies going into them are wasted on something else.

When we clean our minds, and our thoughts, our intellect is clean and we can see clearly, but when our intellect is polluted by sexual thoughts and desires, we can only see this much as the crudity of such desires. In this defect, these intellectuals are usually dogmatic, they lack abstract thinking and hardly innovate, because they lack control over their sexual force. Finally, when we waste this creative power, and especially the semen, we waste that energy that would be converted into what is called the kundalini, and so many other aspects that compliment and even make up the intellect are wasted.

Abilities such as those of consciousness or wisdom, are wasted because the human being lacks the spiritual practice that opens up all these. These abilities, lead humanity to even a greater intellect that was ever imagined, for in this case the intellect is not unidirectional, but omnidirectional, and we can all perspectives, and analyze reality from all points of view, and thanks to this, our intellect is more easily inherently, because of its universal nature, with the truth.

The most influential issue of this uncontrolled sexual energy, is the lack of moderation that comes with it, and the waste that affects the human intellect and potential of the same on so many levels. In fact, it may be proved in the future that intellect is greatly or fundamentally a mere factorization of the transmutation of this sexual-creative force, and that its waste and lacks of transmutation, through whatever channels of the human evolution and genetic make up they may be, will either lead us unto a superior intellect or an inferior one.

When we see this sexual waste, and uncontrolled life, we not only see a psychic, physical or even spiritual way, but we see all these processes and even human nature and path as a whole completely undermined, and the life of the human beings loses its primordial sense. We can deduce, too, that his sexual unrestrained life, is also the product of a lower degree emotional compendium, based upon those of fear, survival and all those things relating to the worst aspect of the humans, led aberrant into an state inferior in moderation even to that of the average animal.

 Therefore, this sexual factor, is also a fear, and survival factor, in which the human being deceives himself to sacrifice one thing for the other, and to falsely believe that there is actually any progress in this sexual disinhibition. The necessity is being confused and mashed up with so many pleasures and dogmas; delusions of the mind that the human being is led into more animality and survival mind that it is needed from him. There are two types of mode or consciousness, that of survival or that of creativity.

The survival mind is one based upon masculinity, upon necessity, constantly seeking food, mate, constantly, seeking, as it is obvious, to survive, it works under an altered metabolism, and thus, such high degree of metabolism, inherently leads to a lower expectancy of life, to less time for the creative or otherwise called intellectual process, for all intellectual process is actually of a creative nature, for even if thinking about the external object, or not really creating, we are obtaining this information through this same creative faculty, and the external perception is integrated to our internal creativity.

The other process, that of creative kind, is more feminine, is more ankled to a lower metabolism, everything is slowed and we have more time, it is more subtle, more dynamic, and abstract. This is the same dichotomy as that of running and that of meditating or relaxing, in one you think clearly, while in other you may think but you still have to maintain the physical aspect to a degree that the mind cannot fully develop. Running, for food, to heed from the beast, to hunt, to collect fruits, etc, is the same survival process as that of the sexuality, except that the sexual process may be called the most subtle of all these survival processes, but because such is the case, it is then the link between the instinctive, or animalistic mind, and the intellectual or human; spiritual, mind.

Therefore, because it is the channel of all these convergences, and even the channel of all dichotomies, of the crude and the subtle, of the material or the spiritual, and because all these things, in their conjunction lead to a higher intellect, it is key to achieve the proper moderation into a natural quantification and expression of this sexual process. For this reason, it is known that many of the greatest geniuses, of all time, like Newton or Tesla, had little if any sexual or romantic desire at all, and so it is known that they may have died as virgins or mateless, this is due to their great intellect, long hours of study with little sleep and higher intellectual abilities being concentrated to such a degree that they not led anywhere else into waste, but naturally solely directed at such superior intellect.

Not only that, but in this lack of mating and sexuality, there is also a certain asocial process, by which there is a natural or even now to themselves tendency to get more distant with people and be asocial, for in this same lack of sexual unrestrained or even romantic one, there is also a great part of the socialization motivation, and when all these are put together, we then not linking with the normal people, who were not as intelligent, but were fragrant in their search of the more cruder aspects of life. We see all these thing correlating, and the more we may evolve, the more clear shall be the image of the direct difference between necessity, fundamentally the sexual one, and the dichotomy between man and animal, intellect and physicality, materiality and spirituality, one seeing all problems and the other one seeing all solutions, one seeing deception and illusion, the other truth and the Creator.

Curiosity is one of the most permanent and certain characteristics of a vigorous intellect.

- Samuel Johnson

3. The Secrets of Psychic Fascination

Whenever you do something, you do it for a reason, no one does anything which they don't like, or with which they are minimally fascinated with. If you go to the cinema, it is because you like the movie, if this was not the case, you would not take the time to go. If you are interested in a particular subject, you take the time to study, you don't care to spend hours and hours studying it because you like.

The same is the case with intelligence. When there is no fascination, when there is no interest, the brain will not use all its powers to acquire this new ability or understanding of any subject. Fascination is not absolute, it is very complex, and has not been very studied. But according to my metaphysical studies, very simply spoken, fascination is what actually leads to energy, to the continuation of any action, and that its start and beginning is begotten by motivation. Without these two,

Newton would have not written his *Principia Mathematica*, and Nikola Tesla would have not spent so many hours a day upon his inventions. On these two, when we think of them, and whenever we think of any person who is a genius, what do we think? There is this image in popular culture that being a genius and being crazy may actually be the same thing, such myth is not very far from reality, if we understand it from the point of view of fascination. When something we like turns out to be true, or when we react to something that we had expected, we often jump, burst into tears or laughter, we may express it in many different ways, but this expression is nothing but the result of fascination.

When we go into these states of hyper, we are often called crazy. What is the difference between the genius and the average intelligent person, if not the degree to which such fascination or craziness has manifested? The only difference is that their degree of interest, of determination, of curiosity, are higher, and that as such, the craziness is seen, as a habit, as a part of their being and identification.

 The scientist who experiments is because he is fascinated with the possible outcomes, with discovering the truth behind nature, to discover a new process of reality. This thirst for knowledge, this curiosity, is the result of fascination, and the higher the fascination, the higher the capacities of the brain and, more importantly mind, to work on such intellectual tasks in the most efficient manner.

Contrary to sexuality, fascination is more psychic than physical, although it has a great effect and control over all material, which may be considered solidified fascination, even so, the control of this quality is mostly mental, while external influences are minimal, although not non-existent. You may say fascination is the pre-stage of the sexual process, for without fascination, there is no attraction towards that other part we would like to share with.

All that sexual process, all that fascination, is the same with intellect. When there is no fascination, everyone may seem to be mentally retarded. We cannot obviate the effect of such fascination upon intelligence, for it is like a car that is judged based on it having no fuel, if the car cannot run, you cannot say it is a bad car, it would be unfair, for it has no fuel and you have not even started it. The same is true for the mind, of which fuel is fascination and motivation. We are all intelligent and skilled, if we like that which we do, but all those who hate their jobs, will most likely end up being poor at it.

Fascination is not absolute, it is relative. People may be good at some jobs, although they may think they don't like it, based on a wide variety of social pressures but even in that eventuality, when a person is fascinated, even unconsciously to anything, they will render higher upon performance and they will be considered better. The cause of such fascination is multiform, it may simply be a reaction derived from past lives, in which a person has already that talent, and they are expressing this fascination once again, or it may be active, cultured from a multitude of polarities within our minds, in which we feel certain fascination with somethings more than with others. Why are some people seemingly better at some things than others, or simply more intelligent? The answer is within fascination.

This fascination is sub-encrusted into their minds, and hence, they are not aware of the effect of the same upon the differentiation of them with others, individually or collectively. Why do students seem to have differing grades on different subjects? Some may be good at math, others at English, others at some other language, others at science, and even others are athletes, yet fail in many other subjects. The only difference is within their fascination, that is very easily explained if we take a look into their spiritual paradigm beyond this present incarnation, and if we are able to decipher the many polarities to which this student, within this spiritual-mental composition, may relate to any subject intellectually at all.

A student may have lived in past lives in Spain, others in France, that explain why some are better at Spanish than French, or vice versa. It also explains why most students are motivated by one specific subject, like Physical Education, because, simply, physical activity is universal in character, contrary to language, culture and sciences and arts, or the outlooks towards the same. This is why, within the factor of fascination, intelligence is so relative, and so dependent upon the mind and spirit of the individual, that guides him/her towards one subject or the other. This may also be the reason, because of which, intrinsically; without the influence of any subject in its entirety, some subjects or types of intelligences may be harder to acquire than others, such as mathematics, or hard sciences, for they are inherently less likable than other subjects. While subjects such as language, or arts, may be more likable and in tune with our interest system.

On the subject-object relationship, some subjects may result more easily for males than for females, for the conjunction of the polarities into such an effect is also different, and the brain is prepared for different types of fascination. So on and so forth, we can analyze each of these differences and see why fascination is the root cause of different types of intelligence. It's not that intelligence makes people curious, but curiosity and our interests is what guides our intelligence.

The key aspect of such fascination is this: that it is beyond our conscious mind, and thus, we cannot choose it, but it is inherent in us in a spiritual context. To direct these forces more easily, we shall have the ability to access our subconscious mind, or command and guide our spirit, so that our interests are guided towards that which we may be lacking in. Even people who suffer from mental retardation, are too, an expression of this karma, in which a person has to pay for the wrongdoings. At the core, or these psychic expressions, are too, the product of fascination, for to commit that wrongdoing, we had to be fascinated, and the castigation is that these levels of fascination and interests are low at the core of the fundament of things, that the person is seen as retarded.

The core of intelligence is that fascination is directed towards these key abilities that set the rest of the intellectual force. If these factors or key abilities are lacking, the person will lack intellect, if they are strong, the person will be seen as an intellectual, or even a genius. Just like the law of Paretto, 20% of the abilities, represent 80% OF WHAT IS CONSIDERED TO BE INTELLIGENCE. This means that the mere difference in intelligence is a subtle expression of subconscious fascination towards basic fundamental abilities that, repeated over time, form patterns and create what is seen as intelligence. But sadly, if the machine is defective from the beginning, the more complex tasks are not possible, and the difference therefore is seen as more extensive than it really is.

The minute of changes could lead to the greatest changes in intelligence, if such subconscious fascination is gripped. The problem of psychic fascination is that it is a very subtle force, and involves areas of psychology that most people have not become aware of. Even so, now you know, genius is the elevated fascination of a person towards that which they love, which may be seen as craziness, as madness, but as they see the truth, they are also seen as crazy by those who don't. For this reason, fascination works directly in relation to all these social patterns, as we behave in society, as that role which we have been provided by the circumstances and our own effort, by all these phenomena, we develop our own intellect.

Fascination has to be taken great care of, because as much as it could develop our intellect, our energy and potential, it could also limit us, and become a dogma, a sort of attachment to one point of view, that may turn to be false, or that may limit the full potential of our intellect, this interest is to be directed in a moderate way, but that doesn't mean that it should be limiting, or that it should be dogmatic. This interest, this ethereal force, is a magical and omnipotent force that is everywhere, and which is intrinsically universal, and just as ecumenic is to be our sense of thinking and intellect, for therein is the truth.

"The mind is sharper and keener in seclusion and uninterrupted solitude. No big laboratory is needed in which to think. Originality thrives in seclusion free of outside influences beating upon us to cripple the creative mind. Be alone, that is the secret of invention; be alone, that is when ideas are born. That is why many of the earthly miracles have had their genesis in humble surroundings."

- Tesla

---

4. The Secrets of Cognitive Isolation

Nowadays, the average person seems to be submerged in a continuous flow of information, from the moment they get up from bed, till the moment they return to it, they are accustomed to always paying attention to some gadget, device that is supposed to entertain them and bring them gratification.

The problem is that this constant state of immersion of the mind is counterproductive, as the cognitive abilities of the mind, especially that of creativity, are destroyed. When you are paying attention all the time to some device, this device will, step by step, and little by little, destroy your ability to concentrate on more arduous intellectual tasks.

You will not be using your brain, but your brain will be used by a third device that will take control over your mind. You will become like a robot, who is self-programmed to participate all the time on this particular task, that does not boost the intellectual ability of your brain.

That's why cognitive addiction, such as the addiction to movies, to series, to videogames, to your smartphones, and these many gadgets are a key component because of which reason like first, the ability to be creative, to reason, to concentrate for long periods of time, to discern false from reality, etc. The subculture, or collective state of mind that is created from these devices is a very damaging one, and it does not allow the brain to develop very far, the brain is captured by the monotony of meaningless variety, and the signals of curiosity, of search for knowledge and reason are annulated.

The mind becomes just like one of these devices, being constantly connected to an outlet, and being programmed by all this content that does not make the person think, memorize, develop their intellect, but only entertains them, or, in other words, makes their mind enter a state of soft contemplation that is solely directed at making them happy in the short term. It is like being addicted to a drug. Once you become addicted, the brain always wants more and more, and it seems like it cannot stop engaging in this activity. Just like drugs, this activity destroys the neurotransmitters of your brain, and psychic fascination is too, destroyed.

What before seemed to bring happiness or curiosity, now you don't care about it, and this is all due to the attachment of the brain to this drug. Imagine the brain is your bicep, when you overwork your biceps, and you don't rest, the muscle won't grow and you will become more prone to injuries, the same is true for your brain. When your brain receives way too much information, it is like a glass of water that you feel until the water rises out of the glass, and falls, the water cannot then be drunk, at such a state you can only sip a few drops of the water, the same is true for your intellectual ability. When too much goes in, not much can come out, in the brain, the creative power is activated when the brain is empty, when its fascination is not the obsessive apprehension to one sole activity, or the any constant activity at all, but its sole power is redundant to the ability of the brain for itself.

The brain must be let by itself, and then it can grow, just like a person, learns and grows better when they are by themselves. When a person is surrounded by others, the person is drained, and they need to rest. Less is actually more, when there are too many people in a closed place, it becomes hot and hard to breathe, when a person is by themselves on the outside, or when they are naked, they feel free. The brain suffers as much as your persona. The brain cannot become subtle, when all its fascination and inspiration comes from the external world.

 The brain must be fascinated with itself, and the knowledge and intellect coming then, towards it, will become just as subtle, for the more subtle the fascination, the greater the creativity, just like God had to use the greatest amount of creativity when he created the universe, for there was nothing else before, otherwise, later, when more things were generated, their cause was not the original creativity, but an inspiration. Sadly, human beings are not perfect like God, and they abuse their will by engaging too frequently into inspiration, or input from the outside, instead of becoming more comfortable at cognitive isolation.

Imagine you are in a concert with a large crowd of people, when there are so many people in one single place, you cannot move, and some people will start experiencing claustrophobia, the same is true for you brain, when there is too much information flowing into the brain, the brain cannot work properly, it cannot generate by itself, and the creative power which was otherwise of tremendous force, is now almost deactivated. When we enter the meditative process, what happens? The mind tries to invert itself, you have to eliminate all distractions, you have to focus on yourself, or in your own thoughts, and not become the victim of the outward thoughts that come from your external perception, the same is true when we sleep.

The internal chatter comes out, because you had too much information processing during the day, and the mind cannot enter a state of sleep, guess the state of intellectuality of the mind is the same that the state of sleep, for in such states the third layer of the mind, the one that brings about the dreams, creativity, and intuition cannot work correctly, and this is the reason why creativity is destroyed on the person that suffers from cognitive overload. Cognitive overload is the mainstream term for the excess of input into our cognition, that is mainly caused by addiction, life circumstances and what not, and that causes brain fog, that is nothing but this state of atrophy of the thinking muscle.

One of the keys to intellectuality, then, is nothing but the opposite of this mental disorder, cognitive isolation. Each of these processes, such as those of concentration, reasoning, thinking, discernment, intuition, creativity, and whatever else, are all due to the fact that each of the layers associated with each of these faculties are being squeezed little by little by this constant flooding of the mind. When there is flood, you cannot go out, everything becomes smeared, and simply you are in a state of pause, the same happens when too much information enters your brain. Too much or too little is always bad, but lack in sex, the less, the more restrained, the better it will be for you.

This is what happens when you stop, for in the material world, for the mind, less is more, and what makes you stupid could actually make you smarter. The smart person would die till they enjoy every bit of this moment of instant gratification, but the smartest people are those that are able to get the most out of nothing, and that find much in very little. Just like there is sexual transmutation, there is psychic transmutation, this process is subtle, but it is possible.

Cognitive isolation is simply another state of fascination and sexuality, for these processes are all related to one another. When we are not connected to the outside, the mind tends to go inward, and then connect to the inner portions of itself, wherein God lives, and there is eternal and universal intelligence. We cannot ask for infinity in the world of materiality, for the many parts cannot ever become one, in this ocean of many ones, but the one can become all of them when it finally meets itself.

 Sleep when you are awake, and you will be awake when you are asleep. To be easily understood: when the conscious mind sleeps and is not constantly being bombarded, the subconscious awakes, and then all the abilities found therein, not only that, but each of these abilities or portions of the mind by themselves become stronger and they can more efficiently attain their maximum potential.

Moderation is the key to everything, including cognitive occupation, but even within such moderation, the extreme levels of isolation are actually positive, if they are done moderately themselves, and they are actually more natural, if cognitive isolation solely means to end the many addictions to smart devices, drugs, people, attachments, and all these occurrences that are so common nowadays. Imagine you are by yourself in a very distant place, where you are free from distractions and preoccupations, would you not be able to think more efficiently, would you not be more creative, would you not be at peace? I think it really would.

Whatever you think, it may actually be the opposite, and where you may think there is boredom, there may be found the greatest of happiness, for the greatest truths are found in happiness, and the truth does not need many words. In the beginning, there was no Creation, yet Creation came to pass, was not the Creator in itself much smarter in isolation than it is by creating all this imperfection, especially human beings.Therefore, perfect your intellect by becoming more isolated, by becoming one within yourself, just like God himself does, and creativity, supernatural abilities of all kind, intuition, memory and all these abilities will flower. What could not come to pass if it was not because you were addicted to falsehood, because you believed the illusion of the material, and all the pain and horrors that come with it. Falsehood is everywhere found when you always seek, but when you don't seek anything, and stay with yourself, you may think it is boring, but guess where you think there is nothing there is actually everything, and everything will you realize, has already been given to you.

16. "What magical trick makes us intelligent? The trick is that there is no trick. The power of intelligence stems from our vast diversity, not from any single, perfect principle."
— Marvin Minsky

5. The Secrets of Meta Cognizance Liability

Metacognition is defined as the ability to think about thinking, to think about, and understand how thinking works, how the mind learns, and according to our points of view, even to understanding how the brain works, so our understanding of this field is wider, far more holistic and integrated with aspects of intellectuality that are applicable by the human beings through the same.

Pedagogy is the means by which we can impart knowledge and explain it in order for the student to understand it in the most efficient manner. Meta Cognizance, contrary to what people may think, is not simply a matter for the teacher, but it also is one for the student, who needs to understand how his brain, and mind works, so that he can better use them. It is very easy to understand through this simile.

When one starts to practice a new sport, or a new martial art, you need to have the foundations of how to play it, or you would be in severe disadvantage, you would need to learn its way and basic foundations, so that you can play against the others with some essentialities. When you play chess, you need to learn how the chess game works, you need to learn the abilities of each piece, the styles of play, the game in itself, etc. The mind and brain are a playing field, or a chessboard, and you need to learn how each of these functions work, so that you can better apply them in real life. There is a tremendous wastage of psychic and neuronal ability when the person does not seek to apply a style of cognizance or learning, when they solely learn by what they have been taught, or through the first thing that comes to their mind.

It is key to understand the mind and brain to the utmost point, so that we can use them to the same degree of fruition. It is especially true that the intellectual ability is one of the abilities that grows inadvertently poor, and that those who think, even those who are supposed to think intelligent, commit the mistake of not being aware about the flaws of their own thinking. This is because thinking, and the intellectual abilities, especially the most abstract ones, are very relative, are very personal to the subject in question, and because of that reason, they are not validated to the other as much as the physical characteristics of a person would be.

 Furthermore, this is the reason why so many of these erudites, who think they know much and understand much, are actually flawed in their thinking, and they are vessels for control by people who are above them. This is the reason that so many intellectuals have been going around in this world, and why they are accepted by the people, even if (1) their ideas are lacking in universality, and thus cannot be applied to many other aspects, because (2) they cannot apply in the practical world, but are only possible in the subjective imagination, or (3) because the idea in itself is flawed, illogical, and has been created solely to persuade the population one way or the other, or by the intellectual solely to gain some recognition and boost their intellectual ego.

In this way, it is clear there is a great problem herein, that these intellectuals, and any person at all, deceives themselves by thinking that they think, and that they are, in their relatively perfect abilities, neglecting their holistic imperfect self, and thus, one consumes the other by their ego and their unconsciousness. This is the problem, not only of these magnificent subjects of exemplification, but of the common person, who lacks the means by which they could think in a most efficient manner, and through which they could learn even faster.

 For this reason, humility is the first step to learning about learning, and to thinking about thinking. There are 3 processes that affect thinking, 3 ways to think about thinking derived from the same, and 9 relationships between all these former processes. The first of these mechanisms that affect it is the physical part of our body, which is the outermost layer, this layer is composed of the many mechanisms that the body uses to envelope and develop our thinking processes. It is built upon hundreds of millions of neurons, that are like little electrical soldiers that communicate with each other, the brain is not only electrical based on the functions of this element within it, but it also because the atoms that form these neurons, and the same being alike the formers, are formed like the atoms we study in the chemistry, the inside part called neutrons are the holders of the information, while the neutrons transmit this information.

 The brain can either be static, when the information does not move very quickly, or in a more dynamic state, when information moves quickly through the neutrons. The brain is divided into two hemispheres that control different sets of functions, the intuitional ones and the analytical ones, while within both of these, and in the proximities of the same, in convergence, there are various parts of the brain of which we don't understand their functions.

For this reason, it is key that we understand how the brain may be turned into a more solid and dynamic machine, so that we may be able to think better. We need to understand the macrocosmic and microcosmic aspects of the brain, of the former being aspects such as the genetic impression upon it, the division of the hemispheres and which is more developed, the flow of blood and oxygen into our brain, the homeostasis of the neurons and neurotransmitters, etc. All these aspects we shall understand better, it is already known, that there are certain physical and dietary habits that affect the functioning of the brain for good or bad. It is very simple, if you take substances that are static, and that are crude, so will occur to your brain, we need to investigate a lot more to understand how the brain works, and how many of these foods may affect it.

We know that smoking and drinking alcohol is bad for the brain, and that it kills neurons, but you need to know that, and this will be better known in the future, there are foods beyond this that hugely affect the brain for good or bad. For example, static foods will destroy your intellect, or foods that come from death, or that have been burned through cooking, will themselves burn your brain and its capacity. Foods like onions or garlic, can also affect your brain, and this is related to the spiritual aspect of it, which we shall proceed to analyze later.

Take a look at what a prominent Hindu philosopher said about onions and their effect on the brain: *"The human brain floats on a liquid called the blood-brain barrier. In the presence of this protective shield, no substance can harm the brain. But the 'hydroxylan sulfone' present in garlic and onion damages this liquid due to which the brain's capacity is greatly reduced and as a result the thinking power of a human being is greatly reduced. Therefore, not only spiritual seekers but also ordinary people should never eat garlic and onion."* (Ananda Marga Darshan). This therefore argues that there are many foods that are known to provoke damage upon the brain, and that they need to be removed from our diet if we want to emerge to the top of our intellect.

 This knowledge, that comes from Indian spiritual philosophy, just as ancestral as present investigation, needs to be added so that we can improve our intellect in the best manner. Just as this one, based on all the previous factors, we are to understand human intellectual ability from the physical point of view, so that we can better understand how our brain works. Onto the next phase, electricity emanates light, just as the brain emanates thought, which is light.

The brain has a plate over which light is reflected, just as the camera, and they are printed in the brain as thought, thinking, is the ability of the brain to discern the truth through the manipulation of these thoughts, which are actually the light as been printed in the electricity and protonic properties of the neurons, the capacity of the brain, or of its electricity to store this reflection is called memory, and remembering is the ability of the mind to bring it back to the thinking plate, to continue its use.

These are the two main abilities of the mind. Now, the mind has various ways of learning, and thousands if not millions of ways to interpret reality, these are the memorizing styles, and the thinking styles, and the many topics it can learn are the pattern over which it deploys its abilities. Memorization is drawn mainly from three abilities: repetition, association and impression. Each individual needs to learn what ability they need to improve, so memorization is improved.

Thinking is too, drawn from various associations, within this ability, the countless logics are the outlooks given to the patterns of the All, which are the intelligences. To improve upon all these abilities, we need to study all these learning styles, and taking into account the other secrets, understand how to conjugate them all under the umbrella of individual practicality and development. The most important of these intelligences, is arguably, meta cognizance, and especially if it is paired with spirituality. Upon this last property of the human mind, is that there is its appearance and the deployment of the deepest layers of the mind upon the same.

The mind has 5 layers, each of them accounting for different sets of abilities and states of the mind. Each of these layers need to be understood in order to draw the best intellectual practices and developments.

LAYERS OF THE MIND

MIND OF DESIRE - KAMAMAYAKOSHA, perceives the world, guided by 5 senses.

SUBCONSCIOUS MIND – MANOMAYAKOSHA- Thinks and memorizes, logical intellect

SUPRAMENTAL MIND-ATIMANASMAYAKOSHA- Creativity and intuitional full-picture intellect

MIND OF SPECIAL KNOWLEDGE-VIJINANAMAYAKOSHA- Special knowledge, deep abstract thinking

GOLDEN MIND– HIRANYAMAYAKOSHA- Spiritual thinking, supreme truths and knowledge; wisdom.

The spiritual stage has to do with these deep layers of the mind that are attained according to the spiritual development of the person. The spiritual development, changes not only the mind, but the corporeal branch, and the inverse is also true. When a person becomes spiritual, all the branches become subtle, and thus the person itself, and every atom that composes his spirit and body, become more ethereal, and less physical. In this state, the consciousness is expanded, and thus the mind is in more affinity, as mentioned in the first chapter, with nature, and acquires greater wisdom.

We are to study these layers of the mind, and the ways in which we can enter them and obtain the treasures therein found. The greatest treasures are found within the deep layers, and these can only be accessed through meditation, and only superficially through arduous abstract thinking and contemplation, which we may be innate in those we call geniuses. Spirituality in regards to intellect, is a deep state that can be attained through our thoughts, for as Jesus Of Nazareth said "Our bodies are what we eat and our spirits what we think", thus, what we think is not only a matter of intellect but a matter of spirit, and the spirit itself, too, affect the intellect and the body, which are all separate by themselves, but one together.

Therefore, we must take the appropriate care of each part of the temple, so that God can live within it, and he may be able to grace us with his divine knowledge. Through the power of the spirit, we can improve the power, or lack of the same, of the brain and mind, we simply need to know of its power, and through auto-suggestion, we can operate even beyond our predisposed defects, we need thus, to learn not to be limited by any of these dogmas of metacognition, and understand this secret from a holistic perspective that integrates body, mind and spirit. Perfection can only be found when we become conscious of our defects through humility, and we re-discover the means by which we can improve all these areas.

"There is a universal intelligence that we call God or Soul or Spirit or Consciousness, and it is everywhere and in all things."

— Wayne W. Dyer

6. The Secrets of Universal Amalgamation

Res universalis veritas est, this is the latin aphorism, by which I start my book concerning truth and deception, meaning; the universal reality is the truth. The truth can only be found within universality, or within any subjective paradigm that is within the inception of the same. Intelligence is, truly, nothing but the search of truth through intellectual means, thus, a person cannot be intelligent that is not under the guidance of the universal paradigm. This paradigm, which is guided by so-called "All", is to be attained through spiritual means, only through spirituality can the mind increase the radius of its consciousness, perception and potential for knowledge. Most of what is defined as intelligence, is not really a greater degree of intelligence, but of knowledge provided by consciousness.

This knowledge is not solely attained by itself, but it has to be rationalized. There is a point where this knowledge is so significant, and has so much weight on the conclusions to be dictated, that by itself, it then becomes reason. No one can become significantly intelligent, that is not guided by this universality. Through intellect, we may understand the subjective microcosmic truths within the world, within the radius of our crude perception, but we can in no way understand those truths that are beyond the relativity of the same, this is only the occupation of the consciousness of the mind.

That is why, the inner layers of the mind, of which we spoke in the previous chapter, can in no way be attained if not through the apprehension of some spiritual development. Intelligence of the crude kind can only reach thus far, but intelligence, that sees the pattern of correspondence and hidden causes and effects between things apparently divergent, is only possible when our consciousness is aligned with all dimensions within our own, and when we see the object and subject as the same thing.

The reason we cannot fathom the truth without concrete crude truth, is because we have not attained such level of spiritual development, as to discern beyond the weight of our own subjectivity in opposition to the embellishments of the All and all its many factors and interceptions. One is linear, one is merely directed at one specific point, the other is radial, meaning, it expands all around our self.

Within such patterns of the deployment of our consciousness, the linear ones are very impotent, and lack a wide range of patterns over which the intellectual envelopment can be fed. Intelligence, and the attainment of comprehension over the object, needs a number of patterns, so that the factors and laws, the how and why, are understood, but if the mind, as it is the drawback of most people, is only directed towards one point of reference, intellect is greatly suppressed and cannot reach its total potential. Universality, therefore, is nothing but a question of consciousness, or of being found in a state of mind or attitude in which the universal paradigms are apprehended and utilized by the mind.

The first stage of this state, all of which are then to lead to the natural spiritual ultimatum of human life, is one of thought, most people only think about one particular point of reference, while they obviate the others, the truth is to be found by looking or thinking unto all references. It is also within the next stage, that of belief, that people may or may not limit themselves in the conduct of these thoughts. They think that there is no relation between two particular points of reference, when there is actually a great connection between them.

They fail to understand that there is a connection among all things found within the universe, all things are connected to each other, all things are driven into the same ultimate goal, and they all come from the same source, then, the truth, and intelligence, at its top form, is one of a universal family. This has to be understood by the people in their belief. If they are led by limiting beliefs, like those of the materialists, the skeptics, and the empiricists, then they will not be directed towards the expansion of their mind, or the subtle-enactment of their consciousness.

Therefore, the belief must be tolerant towards all points of view, all factors and all interceptions. It must know of the laws of correspondence, cause and effect, polarity, etc, and all these laws of the mind-ether, by which they can understand and realize that all things are connected, and that knowledge in its ultimate form, and of the most treasurable kind, is only found within this sphere of reach. Finally, when these two stages and functions of the mind are reached, the ultimate stage is that of emotionality, that is needed to reach the spiritual form of such universal amalgamation.

This is reached by founding this knowledge upon devotion, and love for all things, and for the all itself, and the creator of the same, without such love, we cannot obtain a deeper level of consciousness, for love is the key towards empathy, and empathy is nothing, but (at least in its crude form) a more familiar and short-ranged form of connection or interiorization within the consciousness or nucleus of an external object. Many of the great intellectuals only reach thus far, because they do not love, they lack devotion, they lack purpose, and ultimately, all they do lack practicality, and they could not reach their levels of potential intelligence, because they did not understand the power of consciousness and universal and occult knowledge.

Universality and occult knowledge are one and the same, in a deceived society, where hiding the truth is at the core of the power structure, occult knowledge is the only true knowledge, and all other knowledge is either within the subjectivity of the crudity of the average person, or is practical only in the apparent manner, but when we want to attain the truth, either within the planetary or the universal sphere, we are to attain occult knowledge, universal knowledge, and with the help of spirituality, consciousness, by which these things, and their utilization may be more easily prescribed.

When we understand this, we know for a fact, from this more holistic perspective, that what before was for us a law, or a criterion that cannot be changed, now is a mere opinion, and that which before was an underestimated opinion, now becomes a superior law. Within the relativity of the absolute, is the absolutely relative. This is a law that says that nothing is relative, and that everything is absolute. By this, we mean that nothing is insignificant to anything at all, but everything meets a pattern with all things, and there are no accidents, but only incidents.

Everything is, because everything has got a purpose, everything has got a reason of why it must exist, nothing at all is dysfunctional, everything meets a functions, and the superior function of mind, is only found when no function of anything at all is neglected, and when everything is loved, otherwise, all that which you try to understand, which you try to reason about, will only be understood from a decimal and decimated point of view, meaning, that it will only be showing to you in the .1% of its true nature, and it will only be a minute fraction of how much it could actually mean to you.

The problem of humanity, and more so in regards to intellect, is that their ego makes them believe that they know all things, all that they know for certain what they really don't know, or is completely opposite if they had the consciousness they lack, this is why most people, even the intellectual or geniuses, die, and say they know nothing, because they never knew or understood anything in the first place. First, understand your situation and role within the all, and then try to understand the role of others things, which is basically the ultimate purpose of intelligence.
Not only are you within the All, but the All is within you, understand that no one is free from this great truth, what is somewhere, is everywhere, and you are that thing, you are pure spirit inside a human body. Understand things from this point of view, and the truth will become clear, and intelligence will be hugely increased, but if you only see a possibility, or a reality, then you are limiting yourself and pushing yourself down a pothole. There is nothing that cannot be solved through this mindset, everything is already available, the key is whether you want or not to realize the truth.
The greatest minds were all knowledgeable of this fundamental fact, and that's why they innovated in their respective fields. Universality, innovation and rebelliousness come all in the package. Do not ever think that you can obtain one without the other, you have to be courageous and humble to legitimize your own potential, but if you judge yourself, you will always be ignorant, because that judgment is in itself the proof that you are ignorant, poor in consciousness and a victim of your own ego. You have to get out of your comfort zone, and be more tolerant, not only of the other, but of all things, and understand all things, animals, plants, mineral, and even rocks, even the sun, the stars, the planets, everything, love them and have sympathy and empathy for them, and all the profound truths will be revealed, and your ultimate intelligence will be unveiled. No one can attain such a state that has not suffered much, and understands everything from a humble, patient and courageous point of view, that listens to the unheard, and does limit itself to be deaf to what they hear all the time.

"Intelligence without wisdom is nothing more than stupidity that looks smart."
— Craig D. Lounsbrough

7. The Secrets of Applicative Ultimation

There is a final aspect to all theory, to all invention, imagination, and contemplation, and that is practicality, that is free will, and the ability of the people to choose wisely, what is right; wisdom. In the last chapter we touched upon the topics of consciousness and knowledge, which come hand-in-hand, what concerns us, in ultimate stance, is will and wisdom, the W.W. duet that defines human life and the meaning of it.

This life is a divine comedy, the human being is what he chooses to be, we are thrown upon this world, and we have been given free-will so that we learn the truth, and we may be able to perfect ourselves. Failures and mistakes are the point of human life, and the essence of life is struggle, to just try one more time. In the ultimate stance, no one cannot not be intelligent, it is all a matter of will and wisdom. How many geniuses have not been stupid, and how many stupid people have not done genius or do genius things in some way or the other.

We are all geniuses and idiots, the difference is the will and outlook of the people, through which they see the cosmic accommodation of their intelligence. For example, animals may not be as intelligent as human beings, yet within that lack of intellect, they do just what they have to do, they comply with the laws of nature and they do not break any laws at all. These beings are perfect, and intelligent, even within their stupidity, because they do not speak, and they inherently understand what they ought to do.

The problem of the human being is that he is a slave to his ego, and he believes in the superficial social expectations of the unwise. Intelligence is rather found within righteousness than within intelligence. For one may become benevolent, moral, righteous, divine, and much more while being of a lower-intelligence, but intelligence itself cannot derive into perfection, but at many times it is the same that causes the greatest of imperfections, aberrations and deviations from nature.

 Therefore, will is to be moderated to follow nature, and no matter the intelligence, that being will become intelligent by divine merit, by the subtle blessing of the ever-increase in consciousness and wisdom. While the being that abuses this intelligence, will not be able overcome it, when we are righteous and wise, the intelligence can be overcome, and all things are possible, but by following the crude laws of our ego, we then destroy the full potential to overcome all such barriers.

What concerns is this, that all strength, and all possibility, lies within our will, and within the proper election derived from the same, which is called wisdom. It is said that to succeed, you must fail, then, to become intelligent, you must first be a fool. You have to fail many times, so that you may learn what election is right, you have to become weak in will, so that you then may become strong in the same.

You need to learn, ultimately, what is truly valuable in life, and what is valuable is this: to follow the laws of nature, and by the divine habilitation, to be endowed with the cosmic power to overcome all barriers, and to do so, with these laws in mind, and vice versa. Our righteousness is the measure of our power, and our power is the measure of the degree to which we can apply the same.

Intelligent or not, you need to understand that nothing happens by chance, and that we are all one, and that what you differentiate yourself from others, you may tomorrow become the same with them. All actions have repercussions upon ourselves and upon this global self, and they all adhere to the do what you would like others did to you principle.

 If this principle is not followed, if the right things are not given value in life, namely, the spiritual nature of the human being, and the laws and principles that may allow it, then the whole society will suffer, and the yesterday of one will become the tomorrow of the others, and all people, everyone, without exception, will be impeded from reaching their true full potential. The goal of human life is to grow in this degree of perfection, and such degree does not need intelligence, but rather of wisdom and will, and the ability to intuitively follow what is right, this gut-feeling is what allows us to follow our righteous path. We may not become smart, but we may become perfect, a minimum honesty is needed so that we may be given what is right for us. The cosmic father knows all we need, we simply need to realize what his pleads are.

The measure of our election, and the will we have given to them, is the measure of our perfection, and the overcoming of any barriers of so-called in-born defects within any of us. It is very simple, we need to take the path that leads us towards the treasure, we have to gain knowledge, to take the right path, we must gain consciousness, by making mistakes through the same, or re-gaining to a difference path, we must gain wisdom by learning from the mistake, and must have the will to overcome all these problems no matter what. We need initiative, patience and persistence.

The first has to do with determination and knowledge-wisdom, we must make the right decision based upon our practical and truthful knowledge, we must have patience, which is consciousness, to let the course develop, or to change it according to the circumstances and our relation with the All, and ultimately, we must be willing to persist, to confront the problems that we will face during the course of our lives. Without these three we will not go very far in life, not only in relation to intelligence, but in relation to all things.

We may speak much, we may contemplate and theorize, but if we don't apply what we have learned, if we don't have a clear-cut wisdom, soundness of judgment and discipline, then we won't be able to advance towards what is right for us, none of what is herein written will even matter, for what is not practiced is forgotten. The only difference between one society and the other is that of these factors of election and discipline, which is a habit too.

We are what we choose to repeatedly do, think and say, if we don't pay the proper value and attention to these things, then we will go down and sink. That is why the greatest enemy of intelligence, and of the human being in general is distraction, the greatest price we pay is by not paying attention to time. When we neglect time, we neglect our perfection, we neglect our potential, we neglect the truth.

The greatest truth is that our lives, and everything is temporal, even within the greatest relatives of time. What has been known to have begun at some time, will also end at some time, but because we don't know the birth of existence, of love, and of consciousness, none of these things will end, but will only change form, just as our spirit never ends, but is always changing forms.

 We can do whatever we want, whatever we imagine we can make into reality, but it is only possible if we have the proper will, and the proper wisdom. You can have a lot of talent, of potential. In fact, everyone, in spiritual guidance, has the same potentiality, for the material world makes us all different, while the spiritual world makes us all the same. When we live, we are all at distinct levels of intelligence, but when everyone dies, and everyone makes the face of temporal remembrance, we are all the same. We must, then, die in life, and live in spiritual death, so that our true equivalent and divine potential may become a reality. What we seek is nothing to what we already have.

Realize that you only need to choose yourself, you need to choose the truth within, and do not look for temporal and imperfect substitutes outside. Happiness will ultimately derive into intelligence, for the super-degree of fascination creates the cosmic energy that is within all things, and that is called love, and within it is the truth that makes all things possible beyond our so-called in-born defects.

There is no defect so strong that may not be overcome by that person that knows that truth and applies it, is righteous and moral and helps the other, in the knowledge that he is one with all things, and he needs to do out what is in and in what is out. You can think much about what has herein been written, but if you don't apply it, and you don't try to prove it, none of it will make sense, I challenge the reader of this, to apply all the principles, according to his own criterion that is outlined in this book, he will be surprised, for he will fail many times, but he will eventually realize they are true, he may become a victim to his ego, but he will have tools by which he may finally become the intelligence person they ever wanted to be.

The person that wants, can, but if you don't know, you don't understand, you don't perceive, and you don't choose, then you will not be able to want anything. You are not free to choose, you think you have free-will but you have none, most people are a product of the other, and they do what is being done around them like sheep, most people are slaves to the social order, and above all things, to themselves, you must have the sufficient will to confront the social order and yourself, so that you may be raised above those dogmas imposed upon you, and the degree to which you have believed them, and deceived yourself into the 'I can't" mentality.

From now on, do not doubt, and you will truly become intelligent, ignore completely those who are intelligent, but not wise, for they will say you are intelligent, or they will invent excuses to not become spiritual, but certainly, they will ultimately learn, at the moment of one aspect of decease or the other, what truly matters in life, and they will realize that intelligence is not in complexity of thinking solely, but in the degree to which we simplify it to gain wisdom, obtain the truth, and apply above our own intellectually-complex ego.

Part 2: The Applicative Means to Unlock Intelligence

8. The Applicative Means to Develop Natural Affinity

Everyone can develop natural affinity, it is only a matter of time until your intelligence becomes one with that of nature. The first factor, as it is the situation that is undergoing at this time, is the great amount of technology that is surrounding us. From the TV, to the phones, to the watches, to the refrigerators, now everything seems to be smart, and the smarter the technology, the more stupid their users become. Why is that? Because this same technology, in the context of human practicality, is what is destroying human intelligence, and replacing the human psychic capacities.

Therefore, technology, even at this aspect, is also suppressing human intellect. When people before memorized numbers, now they are not because that is done by the phone, when people before used their spatial and locational intelligence to arrive at their destination, now that is being replaced by their phone, when people had any doubt, they improved their verbal intelligence by looking into books about, and one by one, each human capacity, and the same expression, need is being replaced by some sort of smart gadget. The first step is this, to align your body, mind and spirit to nature. Your body, which has become a guinea's pig for the big industrialists, is being used as the source of their founding. You need to step away from this idea that everything must be smart or consumed by artificial intelligence, because the goal of artificial intelligence, at its core, is to replace natural intelligence, and the natural affinity of human beings.

That is why you need to replace those artificial aspects of your lives with natural aspects, aspects through which your natural intellectual capacity may be expressed. Start by those habits having to do with your health, for they are fundamental for the right functioning of your neurological and physico-psychic factors. Secondly, start to develop those habits around your mind. Think in terms of nature, contemplate nature, think close to nature, observe nature, talk to nature, be like nature, and occupy your mind in the natural aspect of reality.

Ultimately, change your spirit to that of nature, and change your vision of God to a natural one. When we see the average human being, we see someone who decayed to the degree that none of these things are true, the result being, that due to this misalignment he has lost a great deal of his intellectual abilities, and now he is the product of the mere greed of a few individuals that want to benefit from the rest. Human beings are not better controlled than through this artificial intelligence, to the degree that human beings are no longer human but the product of artificiality. In other words, the human lack of control has led humans into its own slavery, there is no greater enslaver in such regards than ourselves. Because the common person loves to be a slave when such slavery is apparently gratifying and pleasing. Humans love to lack patience and get what they want as quickly as possible. And that is the difference between nature and artifice.

The artifice seems to be under a constant burn out and run, for in this imperfection it always needs to change to please the human eye, and because it cannot live longer than their imperfections allow them to. While the natural world seems to be more based upon the long run, upon the appreciation and contemplation of things. There is no surprise, then, in the fact that most of this technology is created to be easy, quick and pleasing, to be repeated time and time again to feed this human addiction towards the mundane pleasing properties of the world. To achieve natural alienation, you have to operate under the rules of the natural principle of nature.

Nature is self-controlled, nature knows herself, and nature has a great deal of patience. Nature never does anything sooner or later than it should be done, nature is there at the right time, to do what is just right. When we are one with all these laws, we will be one with nature, in whatever area it may be. Just like you need to go to bed at the right time so the physical part of your intellect works right, so you need to pay the right amount of time and attention to nature so you may be able to understand it, and that your intellectual capacities may become one with it. The same is the case when God has a natural plan for you, but you don't listen to it. Because you lack all these sets of intellectual abilities that are provided by natural perfection.

Therefore, in your everyday life, everything you do, must come under the jurisdiction of these laws. Take care that all you do is ruled by balance, by adaptation, by consciousness, by empathy, etc. If you defy just one of these principles, you will destroy your natural affinity, and that idea and intellectual ability that you could have improved or obtained would not be available to you.

Through experimentation, try to comprehend and copy nature, and to learn her wisdom, so you may gain her intelligence. But if you don't understand beyond your own pleasure, your intelligence will never reach its potential, your intelligence will always be assimilated into the frenzy of human imperfection, especially after the fact that you are a victim, not even of yourself, but in parts of others, that know the truth, and that take advantage of you in such way. When you learn, do not learn from human will, do not learn from the laws of humanity, do not be led into ostracism by the laws written in books, or even the opinions, or expressions of emotion or belief, for in them there is the sole expression of human imperfection, and misalignment with nature. To align with nature is to become an attendant of an empty party, where the host is God, the guests are you and the truth in plain sight.

 The truth is already out there, it is you that are lost in your own lies. Nature, that is your best friend, and that reveals God to you, has the answer to all your questions. There is more gained in the empathy and consciousness of nature than trying to control it or make any use of it. The more you use nature, the more you will become a slave to yourself, but the more you let nature be herself, and you become a slave to her, you will become your own God. This may seem like a spiritual aphorism or supposition, but it is too an intellectual one. As so does the spirit manifest in nature, so does the intellect, for the mind is the Temple of God and God is the supreme intelligence hidden in all things. If you become the slave to one, but only one of these natural products, given your own defective will, you will then become stuck in only one phase of nature, you will become addicted to it, and then, your intelligence will become stagnant, and grow no more. Natural affinity must be universal, and look into all perspectives for the natural object that it represents.

Nature is always there to give us all knowledge and understanding, but we lie to ourselves so we may not understand it and receive it. It is all due to human ego, leave behind your ego, become an animal, and solely use your intellect to think of nature, by nature, and for nature, and then all things will be revealed to you without any further complications. Sometimes the most simple experimentations and contemplations of nature lead to the greatest realizations. The problem is that we intend to understand nature with these things which are made by the human hand. How can the imperfect human hand understand and get any truth out of perfection? In our nakedness, in our innocence, in our pristine thought patterns, is the best way by which we may communicate with nature, just as animals do.

All these laws are out there, and they are not subjective, they have no preferences, although humans may think these laws work exactly the same way for all people, they are non exclusive but all inclusive. Nature is all and all is nature. There is no pattern or logic that cannot be comprehended by it. When we apply nature to our artifacts, these become intelligent and perfect, but when we apply artifacts to nature, we betray ourselves, and nature becomes and gives us only the imperfect intelligence we gave to her. The light of nature is the light of perfection, and the light of truth, but the human light is the light of darkness, of deception and of imperfection.

One leads to idiocy, the other, to supreme intelligence. One embraces our potential, the other destroys it. Simply understand and reapply these paradigms, into the context of human practicality, and all reason will manifest before you. But if you only apply yourself to nature, and you become greedy and selfish, if you are consumed by your ego, nature will never provide anything to you, for you are blind from the start. If you don't feel right, other aspects of you, including those affecting intelligence will not feel right. If you already are lost, why don't you take the right path of nature, and begin nature towards the purification of your intellect?

Nature always hugs you, even when you think she abandons you, nature is always protecting you, but it is you who doesn't. If something is not right, if something doesn't feel good, it is not natural, and you are betraying yourself, because you are also a part of nature, and not applying nature is not applying the right intelligence, and not learning from nature, is leading you nowhere. Thus, learn from nature in the most practical and universal perspectives, and do not forget to follow her laws on all these areas leading to your peak intellect.

9. The Applicative Means to Transmute Sexual Energy

Fortunately for us, and as it is evident in its now presented practicality, sexual energy is not uncontrollable, and much has been said about its transmutation. Well-known books, such as "Think and Grow Rich" by Napoleon Hill, have stressed the importance of such a transmutative process for the acquisition of wealth and the general progress of the human being in the material world. Now, it is clear that this force can also be transmuted into intellect, as we explained in the previous chapter concerning this secret.

For such ends, you will have to grow conscious of the fact that the primary motor behind such forces is a physico-mental conjunct. We are to have a minimum control over the hormonal secretions in our body, and the means by which they lead towards this sexual necessity. We shall never confuse desire of the mental type, by a physical propensity that is exuberant given its uncontrolled state.

To transmute the sexual into the intellectual, we need awareness of our thoughts, beliefs and emotions. Each of these factors of the human mind have a lot to do with the sexual connotations of human life. Because, at the core, the sexual component of our lives, is a creational one, it may be hidden in various subterranean forms in each of these thoughts, otherwise thought to be normal, and typical. We need to look out for the most minimum scapegoats or gateways of the natural thinking process, that is more aligned to the intellectual nature of the human being, and that process in which our thoughts, emotions and beliefs are not controlled. So many people in this world are subjected to addiction, whether it be to phone, drugs, alcohol, or sex itself itself in its many manifestations. It could start as a mere curiosity, but it could turn into an aberration, for curiosity turns humans into beasts, but also beasts into humans.

Therefore, in this curious state you should guard yourself against its many endings. Do you want to live an immoderate life, in which your sexual propensities take control of you, and you become a slave, or do you want to take control of them? To pursue this way of life, we are to secure very important factors to the same. The first, of which is, you should develop mental discipline, which is nothing but the discipline you have to control your thoughts, when your thoughts are clear, and they are clean, your intellect will be clear and clean, but when your thoughts are uncontrolled, and you become a slave to the pleasure of the illusory mundane world, your intellect will be shadowy and foggy.

 You will not be able to see the truth, or even be able to reason, for the reason and intellect of the human being are destroyed by the aberrant will of the same, that turns him into a sub-beast. Therefore, all these things account for the transmutation of your sexual energy into intellect. If you believe that sex is everything, then sex will populate every phase of your life, in every waking day, through these beliefs, so together with your thoughts, you need to control these beliefs. The beliefs are mostly limiting and materialistic, you need to change them for unlimited and spiritual beliefs, those that by their very frequency will elevate your intellect.

A third step of the process regarding your intellect, is that you should take care of your emotions, for these emotions are the most directly influenced by the hormones in your body, and they are the gate between an animalistic or humanistic perception of sex. When you don't control these sexually-conjuncted emotions, you will do the imaginable for sex, you will not restrain yourself, and your consciousness, which is a great part of your intellect, will be damaged. If you go to a certain place, meet certain people or at a certain time of the day or month, you shall fall prey to the circumstances, but you shall be at the control of all these situations, and translate the sexual energy into psychic energy. By controlling your emotions a great part of the hormonal process will be controlled.

 This last process is to be controlled by deepening your study of the human body, and the many glands and secretions deriving therefrom by which all these propensities take place. This neuronal and biopsychological process is very important, for it can turn you either to mere mundanity or towards higher elevated thoughts.

Understand the sexual-neuronal axis of the human body, and how they affect each other, and finally, how they impact your behavior, and make you act one way or the other. You should find ways not only to restrain it, but to transmute it in the right measure for the amount of restraint, for otherwise the restraint will lead to sexual repression and an even greater exposition of these lower-propensities of the sexual kind.

Especially, this sexual energy, shall not merely be of the intellectual nature, but of the spiritual kind, so that in these various spiritual activities, such as spiritual music, chanting, meditation, walks, retreats or any of such, you will be able to transform this energy from explosive to implosive, and from a mere waste into the mundane to the Supreme. You should become minimally aware of all these processes, but in this awareness there shall not be an obsession, for otherwise, somehow, the cure or healing process will become a suicidal process.

It is enough that you know, but awareness shall never become a conscious process, but a subconscious one, there is no better medicine than the deepening of our awareness through a subconscious process. The reason for this is that the conscious mind is very linked to our will, and our will, is, most of the time, imperfect, but when our will is directed towards our inner-self, as such is the case in the meditative and spiritual process, we are able to subtle this will as it enter more subtle layers of our mind.

For the more subtle our thoughts, and our will, and our awareness, in this case, of the sexual, and other related processes related to our lower instincts, the more the subtle and natural directive we take over it. But, if this awareness, that has as its precedence, the intellectual transmutation of this energy, becomes a rather conscious process, the mind will fall victim to mental habituation, and what before was mere care, now become pre-occupation, and bad-being.

The fight must be subtle, it must be natural and flow like the river, from your inner-self, it must not become abruptly and under wrong pretext and pretense. When sex is the mere thinking of your life, it will become meaningless, and you will go nowhere. Many question the reason behind their lack of intellectual ability, and they would be surprised how related it is to the sexual energy and the many ways in which it inhabits the gateways and shortcuts between these different layers of our self.

The question of intellect is also a sexual one, for the more a generation of human beings control their sexual force, the more the probability that their very self and even their genes become sexual, rather than intellectual. You are fortunate to know the great power of our sexual energy, and that through, you can take greater control of these limitations of the biological kind. You should also be able to control your lower-propensities, connected to this instinctive self, that is fearful, ever-worried and seeking survival.

You need to lower all these points, to ground yourself, so that you may find peace at nature and your own Creation, substitute this survival sense that you may display, by Creative sense, fear and conformism is lack of creativity, the more creativity you become, that more opportunities you can see to grow and transmute this sexual energies and needs, or other instincts into a powerful intellectual force.

The more clear your thoughts and beliefs, the more clear will your subconscious mind become, and the greater will be the control over your sexual and therefore, your intellectual potential. Say to you that you are the ruler of all these forces, and that you do not merely waste them in the mundane and material world, but that you righteously and in all your honor and dignity use them diligently in the reproductive process, and for the betterment and evolution of your psycho-spiritual capacity.

Nothing is impossible if you have control over the infinite power of your spirit, and if you command all these forces through your own deeper mind, do not fall into materialistic conformism, and all the dogmas that certain people that want to undermine human nature and potential tell us. Everyone has the potential to better their intellect through this transmutation, it is not impossible, and it is not reserved for men, it is also for women, it's not only for whites, or light-skin humans, but also, and most importantly, it is, too, for the betterment of the dark skin ones.

All these mental colors, all these dualities, shall be removed when the sexual energy becomes the union of your lower self to your Higher Self, that is directly the intelligence of God, and that has infinite cognitive ability, and you stop being the mere union of a reproductive waste product. Practice these exercises, and configure your life according to these principles, that you should control your sexual energy and primal necessities into an intellectual form of transmutation and elevated thinking, and that thanks to this same capacity, your quality of life will improve, and will be able to achieve not only higher intellect but higher qualities that work for your evolution as a soul.

10. The Applicative Means to Harness Psychic Energy

The good news is that we can take control over this force, we can direct what best satisfies us. We can develop fascination with something, even beyond our predetermined spiritual destiny, if this is not the case, then we are saying that all our interests, and thus our skills are all predetermined, and we cannot change this interest even a bit, but this is not true. The interest, or force of fascination, is a weapon, a tool, we can harness. Just like we can use water, air, fire, or earth to make our lives easier, so we can use this ethereal force in the way it is the most convenient to us. This force cannot be any other than the ethereal force, ether is recognized as one of the primordial elements, how is it not possible to harness this force, if it is natural?

Of course we can, the problem is that society has been trained to develop a state of oblivion over the power of this force on their lives, or of how they can direct it to best improve on whatever they want. As long as we have something to do, as long as we have a soul purpose, we are going to have some sort of interest, this interest can take many forms, some are good, some are bad. It is key, first, that these interests shall not be immoral, shall not be static and of a negative nature, for they will lead to a state of lower psychic abilities, and they will create this force so in a future life, we may develop it. All negative fascination will end up killing your consciousness, and you will go back to plant or rock, want it or not. So the first fundament, is that all this interest shall be vested upon the righteous.

Morality, helping others, protecting and feeding nature, taking care of animals, and of these activities are practices that lead us closer to God, and thus, to intelligence. Eliminate or transmute all those negative interests, that, although they may not directly affect intelligence, they will indirectly turn your intelligence towards the negative side. Habits such as smoking, taking drugs, eating meat and blood, especially in excess, killing others, insulting, judging others, raping, acting against the will of others, and anything that may make the other suffer, will destroy your intelligence.

 That is the reason why so many of these so-called intellectuals had ideas that were apparently splendid, but through their habits we can see how imperfect the fruit of such seeds will become. They smoked, as it is seen in many of their pictures, they were immoral and some of them even committed homicide, at the end, their ideas were not very practical, and ended up being hallucinations and delusions, meaningless brain-racking.

When we direct this force towards negative habits, we act in manners that will not align with intelligent fascination, so we will be aligning with the wrong type of fascination. There are two types of fascination, crude, dynamic, or subtle. The crude one is all that is purely negative and will conduct towards deception, towards immorality. The dynamic is all that, especially the vicious life of the addict and party-goer, that although it may not hurt the other, the intellect and psychic fascination is in a state of exacerbation, and so the mind cannot work or decide to choose between truth or false, the subtle fascination is the one directed towards the moral and the truth is the aftermath. See how each mind is related to many of the other secrets, like those of sexuality. The cruder the fascination, the more sexual, and therefore, no matter the strength of the fascination, the energy derived from it will be wasted on sexuality.

The same is true for any other factor or area of life. Through this fascination, we can either enter a creative mode or a survival mode. Are you fascinated with the subtle or with the crude? For the degree to which you are inclined towards one or the other, is the degree to which you are deceived or into the truth, and the potential you use. Notice how when you are fascinated by the crude things, your intellect always lowers and you are more prone towards animality, while the fascination with the subtle, will lead towards intellect. The key difference between one and the other, is that this crude fascination can hardly be directed, can hardly be commanded to our favor, for the fascination is not created by us, but rather by the intrinsic fascinating nature of this object.

Simply, when we direct our attention towards this force, the object in question does not require thinking for us to be fascinated to it, this is very much how the sexual fascination works, it is a crude fascination that does not require thinking, that the mind is simply in an extraversion state in which we have no true control, for it is more of the outer-suggestive kind. When the power of the fascination is so strong, our will is contaminated, and we cannot direct our false desires, so we cannot direct this force to the degree or direction that we want. On the other hand, the subtle object of fascination, is one that requires more thinking, that needs curiosity, or else this knowledge will not process and the fascination will not enliven our minds.

When you create something, when you have to solve a problem, when you discover something new, or in any other of these actions in which you have to think, the action is a potent propeller of our intellect, the fascination is more subtle, and you can take more control over it, you cannot use this fascination and see it being developed in other areas, while the more crude fascination cannot obtain this very easily. When this is the nature of the fascination, we can direct it to our benefit, we can extrapolate to other areas in which our fascination is not so strong, and one will override the other.

It cannot be solely solely motivation and fascination, it must be both, for both are needed, you may use any to propel the other, but this force of interest must be there, so that one energizes the other. You may not have a particular interest in any given subject, but you can use the power of another interest to work as a vehicle so that this low-fascination interest may be energized. It is like creating a new car model, the new car has not structure yet, and you don't know what fuel it will use, you just need to find the structure, or patterns that assimilate to one of these others interests of yours, so that the affinity is created between object or subject, or you have to energize it through some other interests of yours.

 This interest needs not to be your favorite subject, it doesn't have to be related, simply find a creative way to relate one with another, so that this other subject may become easier through this vehicle. The channel through which you learn, and acquire this ability, must have the blueprint of that particular interest of yours. You must change that which you don't like, so that you may like it, you have to change its structure, and this doesn't necessarily change the truth within it, or the inherent logic of that science or intellectual ability. For example, if you are going to learn a new language, do things you like to do, read comics, listen to the news, read books on whatever subject you like, converse with people you would like to be friends with, etc.

The problem is that language learning is not embedded in motivation, as most of the other subjects at school, and thus, what happens, that the students get bored in class, they hardly pay attention, and after a few years, they forget all that boring grammar that they were FORCED TO LEARN.

See, herein is the difference, fascination is not forced, fascination is natural, the mind works naturally when there is fascination, just as the water flows smoothly on a clean river. For this reason, it is not that these students are not intelligent enough, but that the teachers have not created interesting or fascinating classes for the students, hence, the students are neglected of this basic force by which their mental abilities are to be propelled. Anyone may be seen as retarded or as a genius in two different occasions or subjects, and no one would know why, as long as this force is not given its right importance.

Time and space, also play a huge, role, when a person is in a circumstance they don't like, when they are surrounded by people they don't like, who is always in a bad humor, who is so serious about everything, when a person is inside a cubicle-like prison, without the light of the sun, air, having to go there since the very morning, that person will be negated of their natural interest propensities, so even if something is interesting, their mind, and the very circumstance sets everything upside down. In conclusion, this force is ignored, and the result is the current state of schools, and the educational system, the genius and genius is only developed either alone, or working with a private tutor, and the classes with others ought to be minimal.

For, if everyone has different interests, everyone has different intelligences, or forms to learn, and thus, everyone needs to be taught in a different way. The most important thing to be though is the power of transmuting their interest or fascination towards that which they like, and how the harnessing of this force will empower humanity to finally advance in the more psychic stance of their potential. If you don't feel intelligent, do not worry, just work for that which you like, and use it as a motor for any subject you don't feel interested about, use metaphors, comparisons, stories, familiarities, memoirs, stylisms, and much more so that you can finally transmute all that interest-force, and attune your intelligence into the universal and natural unlimited.

11. The Applicative Means to Master Cognitive Isolation

To be alone is a hard task, the average person is not able to stay a very long time ago, they always seem to need more than they actually do, they deceive themselves to create a false necessity that does not actually exist. People always want someone by their side, they want to feel safe, they want to feel like they have support, because they lack inside. To fill this emptiness, they do not only seek a personal life-mate, but a psychic one, and this occupation of the mind seeks that. People do almost all they do, not because they actually want to do it, but because they don't know how to overcome the challenges of the environment, and thus they pretty much become subjected to it to the point of slavery and desecration of their true selves, which is also their true potential.

As long as the average person needs the outer, the other person, they will never be themselves and thus they will not ever become perfect, and their intellect will not develop very much. Intellect is developed much faster when the mind is in solitude, when it is free and without any distractions and third-objects that may destroy its clarity of discernment. You must free yourself from this false and constant need of needing to feed your mind, just like the false feeling that you need to eat all the time, the stomach gets too filled, and it hurts, it congests and it can even provoke your death, the same is true for your mind.

The more the connection that the mind has to make throughout the day, the more the challenges, the more the pain and burden of emotions, the whole body is then affected, neuronally and metabolically, one thing leads to the other and the capacity of your mind is greatly diminished. You need to spend more time by yourself, especially in relation to the other secrets we have shared with you. You need to spend more time alone in nature, and learn how nature works. You need to speak to the invisible angels of nature, and they will increase your intelligence and they will make you accustomed to feeling fascination with the invisible, with the subtle intelligence of all.

Spend time by yourself exploring your life questions, including those of sex, but make sure that these questions and experiences are natural, and rather spiritual and natural than materialistic and artificial. Make sure that this does not lead to addiction and that it is highly controlled, exploring your will power, for the greater the will in time of temptation the greater the will of the mind that could be directed towards intellect and towards your power of concentration.

Be fascinated at these factors and in general, to any factor that is not either people, drugs, food, or anything other than those things relating to the intellect. It is especially important that this cognitive isolation shall take into account any inspiration, so reading books, or studying, is too, not allowed. The only thing allowed is that you should have a notebook, painting sheets, or any other instrument through which you can record your ideas and, thereafter, get inspired not by the external but by yourself. Be sure to get into a creative/self-inspirational state in which both the internal and external become one, and to the point that these factors develop, through the subtlety of their ethereal essence, a relationship with your mind, so that they may want to reveal all these secrets with you.

 The hidden key is that solitude is the greatest state of friendship or brotherhood, in this state, the truth is revealed, not through the opinion of some mere individuals, but through the opinion of God, that is hidden within nature and yourself. This is like those religious teachings, who say that nothing is better than God, and that he is your only true friend, the same is true for the intellectual question, your true intellectual friend is yourself and nature, your own relationship between you and the All, and not towards any microcosmic entity.

The best form of intellect, is not the one in which a society is surrounded by technology, but by nature, do not be grounded to the cement, to the artificial lights, etc, but try to be grounded towards the grass, towards the sunlight, feel the breeze, feel each atom of nature touching you. Go to the beach, in some far away place in the mountains, very far from civilization, or live and choose a moment at your home where you can be by yourself, and become adapted to having no disruptions to your thinking, to receive no information, except your own voice, and that which comes out of their will become the truth. If you are addicted to any of such information, and are suffering from overload and brain fog, try to cut all these gadgets, especially the smart digital gadgets, that would destroy your neurotransmitters and fascination and motivation from your brain.

For example, if there is any activity you do with that device, try to replace it with an analog device, like a watch, or a device that although digital, is not that smart, and expressive, the less expressive in information the device, the less the cognitive overload that you will suffer. Stay away from cheap forms of entertainment and music, do not become addicted to music, like some people that cannot stop listening to music, watching videos, playing games,etc.
Of all sources of information, the worst of them all are the ones that take into account the most channels of input. For example, a movie or videos, take 3 channels of input, the visual, the auditive, and the verbal. This is a lot of information at the same time, so the brain is flooded and all the negative effects occur, replacing it with reading or sources of information that are not so addictive. The worst of them all are those smart devices that are made to create a social gratification state inside your brain. The best are those that are rather simple, and usually, the older ones are the ones that flood the brain the least.

For example, instead of reading on your smart device, try reading a paper book, see how the more natural the device, the more simple it becomes and the less the chemistry and fascination of your mind is affected. Instead of listening to music with your smartphone, try listening to it through an MP3 player, if you want a timer, do not use the one on your phone, use a clock for that which has that function. The worst of all is the new social media trending, for therein masses and masses of fast content are created each day, and their only purpose is for you to release all those chemicals, similar to a drug.

The smartphone is one, if not the worst offender of the cognitive resistance of your brain, because it artificially replaces many functions that before were natural and because it is too accessible and makes all these addictive content so available to anyone. In general, the smartest and the more artificial the device, the more it destroys the input resistance of your brain, and the more easily your brain is overflooded. You can enjoy all these things, but it would be better if you did without the addictive attachments to all these artificially manufactured devices. In general, let your input be a natural one, or at least one that resembles nature. Take into account the effects of each of these forms of input for your brain, and how they affect each of your abilities. For example, if you watch too many videos, it is possible that your visualization or creative visualization is destroyed due to your brain being flooded in that respect, the same may be true for music, or whatnot.

Inspiration is not everything, the first artists or scientists didn't need external inspiration, like it seems everyone wants nowadays, but they got all their inspiration from themselves or from nature. Operate in the same manner in regards to people, leave people who are known to be superficial or who want to take control over your persona, who are obsessed with you, or who make your mind become preoccupied, for this is especially damaging for your intellect.

The same is true for any substance that changes the plasticity of your brain, like food, drugs, etc. Stay away from them, and let nature and spirituality be your soul of these chemicals. Remember, as a last note, that moderation is key, from time to time, allow yourself to use your smart devices, or that if they are anyhow used, they are used for your own benefit, to achieve something specific, and that you may not become addicted to them. Use them to achieve your goals, not that you may be used by them, or by those who have created these things. You may see certain changes, even in your personality, as the bio-psychological changes start to take effect, do not worry and proceed, for as long as possible, the brain usually adapts to habit in 21 days, and these processes in your brain, are too, attached to habit, so we can guess that habit and brain processes are one and the same.

Therefore, try to convince yourself of challenges, to see how this change of cognitive diet feels, and that you will realize that you feel more satisfied, enthusiastic about the small things, minimalist, natural and as yourself all around, than when you were addicted to the external. When you stop the external attachment, you become yourself, and in this true self of yours you will see certain changes, you may have certain thoughts, increase in intellectual abilities, creativity, intuition, understanding of certain concepts that before seemed difficult, interest may develop for news sciences, etc.

Do not become impressed by these changes, try to be as calm as possible, and be composed, for you may adopt certain attitudes from time to time, do not let these change your perspective, and return to your moderate, yet new natural self once the readjustment occurs.

12. The Applicative Means to Control Metacognizance Liability

The path to apply these principles may not be an easy one, it may not accord with your culture or lifestyle, but truth doesn't know of opinions of subjectivity, either you do what you ought to do, or you will not get to do what you need to do. First, you need to take care of the biological aspect of this process. You need to eat, drink, exercise, and sleep right. You need to do it in the full knowledge that these things will benefit your brain performance one way or the other. You need to gain awareness about the effects each of these, and everything has upon your intellect. You can gain this knowledge by observing results, by experimenting with nature, by personal experience, etc.

Your diet, shall not be made of dead food, but with that enliven you, and it shall be natural, and you shall eat things just as they come in nature, you shall not refine your food, for this will destroy your intellect, if you destroy the food you eat, this food will destroy your intellect, if you kill it, it kills you. You also need to take care that this food is not addictive, for thereafter it will affect the neurotransmitters of your brain. Food can either act as poison or potion for your brain, choose carefully, then, what to ingest. The greater the odor of the food, the more crude and dead it is, and the more it will destroy your intellect, the lesser the smell, the more subtle it is and the more it will enliven your intellect.

Certain ailments contain chemicals that affect the brain for good or bad, you need to identify these, and you choose to moderate them according to your individual case. Do not drink alcohol or take drugs, for these will all equally kill your brain and turn you into an addict. Your brain will not be able to function correctly, it is better to prevent all these things than to go through a healing process. All artificial foods will make your intellect artificial, and you will always think about materialistic ideas or concepts, while natural foods will align you with divine intelligence. Water shall also be as pure as possible, and free from intoxicants. Sleep shall be aligned with the cycles of nature, do not sleep too much or too little, but be as aligned with nature as possible and little sleep will become much. Eat just what is right, focus on the quality of what you eat and drink, and you won't have to eat or drink much. The brain can get injured due to a variety of reasons, risky jobs, risky sports, risky stunts, they all have the potential to damage your brain, or even to convert you into a genius.

Famous are those who have gone through a brain injury and have come out of them as genius, and their intellect changed completely. We are to study how these modifications of the structure of the brain can be done without causing secondary damage, yet achieving the same degree of change. Peace and war must be two wings that support brain development. Be careful of what air you breathe, and of how you sleep in general, sleep and breath through your nose, and develop breathing exercises through which the maximum amount of oxygen can reach the brain, even in particular to that area which you want to potentialize or use in that precise moment. Stay far away from the cities, from places where there is a high degree of pollution and destruction of the natural habitat.

The closer to nature you live, the fresher the air will be, and the environment will be more electric, more positive, and thus the brain will thrive therein. A place where the opposite is true, will only kill your brain, and your health in general, and you will present intellectual problems from a young age. The same is true for radiation, electromagnetic waves and so many other secondary effects caused by technological advancement. The mental aspect is too, very simple, there are books, tools, and much more that present mental exercises. There are very simple exercises you can ideate yourself or follow for others to develop each of these specific mental abilities. Concentration, attention, abstract thinking, visualization, rationalization, discernment, etc.

The best you can do is to operate under your own methods because they will be the ones that work the best for your individual case, no method works for everyone, for we are all different, as explained in the other chapters. Read, listen, become aware of your intelligence, of the nature of reality and of how you think within it. Do not base your intellect and mental abilities upon what others have done, do not be a follower, be your own leader, and your natural intellect will arise. Do the best to understand how the brain and intellect works, observe what has been proven, do not be led by dogmas, escape from dogmas as much as possible.

Do not understand intelligence from one point of view, but from many different points of views. Do not think that there is only one way to the truth, always take into account the alternative and holistic perspective, escape dogmas, religious, intellectual, or otherwise.

Utilize the power of visualization, you can develop it through the other secrets we have presented here, practice your mental and intellectual skills everyday, make it a habit of yours. Do not think that there is only one set of practices or methods, you can invent your own methods to operate all these things. Know yourself, know the principles I have spoken of, and know the subject-matter.Memorize taking into account your way of learning, memorize taking into account your interests and the ability of your brain. While you try to improve in the psychic sphere, remember the impact of the physical arena, subtle causes can have a huge effect upon your brain.

Do not take anything as granted, there are many ways in which a person can learn, do not limit yourself, do not ever think that you cannot improve, that you cannot learn, for life is a constant inflow of these things. Organize your own methods and write them down, build a set of habits according to your individual situations and your intellect will flourish. You will realize that many times you only missed a proper habituation to that task, that is all, you need nothing else, excellence is within habits, and just as the piano man played for 10.000 hours to get expertise, so you must be able to practice every single day your intellect, or it will decay and atrophy. Your brain and your mind are like a muscle, if you miss a day, you will not get the results you want, the same is true for your intellect.

 Be open to all points of view, never become a fanatic of any author, for the truth is in itself and beyond the individual. Take too, into account the effect of your mind over your body, and the power of your subconscious mind, of your creative power and the infinite power of your spirit and faith. If you believe something, it will become a reality, watch out for your emotions, for your beliefs and your thoughts, for they create your life.

 As you believe, so it is. So, do not ever believe that you are lacking any intellectual ability, or that you lack knowledge about how to improve your intellect. Say to yourself everyday, before sleep and just after waking up. 'I am an intelligent person that is always obtaining the truth, and uses his abilities to help others". "I know what intelligence is and how it works, and I know how to improve my intelligence, because it is building up everyday".

Never say to yourself that you are stupid, or anything around that matter, always tell yourself you are the smartest person in the world. There are no limits for God, except for those who think otherwise. Ask intelligence to your own spirit, and you will receive, and intelligence is not absolute, intelligence can come in many forms, and it is beyond the mere intellectual power of anyone.

 Ask your subconscious, and take a spiritual and abstract look into reality, through your intuition, so that you can obtain the meta cognizance knowledge that you know will open the doors of intelligence and wisdom to your persona. Never let the spirit of another person interfere with your capacity, do not listen to what society thinks, listen to the truth, and if there is a knowledge that you have seen has been proven, and improves your intelligence, so it is, and there is a subtle way in which such occurrence takes place, do not listen to the society, do not even listen to the so-called experts, for they only seek their own benefit, for no one, even less so in power wants to see you understand the truth. Understand and seek the truth, and knowledge about intellect yourself.

 Practice meditation, of which we shall present a form at the end of the book, not only to improve your intellect, but to improve your spiritual development and the degrees to which you can potentialize the hidden power of your mind. It is said that we only use 1% of the power of your brain, guess, what, that power is the power of the pineal gland, that gets activated through meditation, and just this part of the brain no one knows its reason, so many other parts of the brain will become activated when you live a spiritual life.

There is no way to achieve the whole metacognitive knowledge and fully activate the capacities of the human brain, if it is not through regular spiritual practice. This is not an opinion, but an undeniable fact. When we attain this spiritual state in mass, society will become smarter than ever, and you will be able to discern the subtle effects of spirituality upon intelligence. The cosmic intelligence knows, and you also know because you are her. All that knowledge is already inside you, you simply need to realize it.

13. The Applicative Means to Integrate Universal Knowledge

No one is born knowing, it is said to us from a young age, no one is free from learning, our life is a continuous learning process. To apply this to your life as an individual is a really arduous task, many think they are learning, but that which they are learning is default and predisposed by the external conditions of the social order, and not by their own particular curiosity. Therefore, when everyone learns as much of the same subject, everyone is just as ignorant of those subjects which are ignored. These ignored subjects are the ones that free the human being, and lead them into their special path of escape, or salvation. But if all students of the All, learn the same from him, then the knowledge is not universal anymore, and based upon deception and the occultation of knowledge.

 The simple solution to this problem is to become a self-learner, to understand that you need to learn by yourself, that you need to develop your own curiosity, your own likes and dislikes, your own path, and that knowledge shall not be vested upon your persona. Learning without election, or freedom of understanding and creativity, or the means by which we can prove the understanding of a problem by our own scheming of the subject-objective pattern, is like a form of slavery like that of dogma, in which the intelligence of a person is not judged upon the relativity of his modus of understanding, but he is cornered to think and understand reality in a way in which he is most easily controlled.

Allow yourself to not believe any of these social dogmas that are created to enslave your mind and will, understand reality your own way, and learn your own way. Do not limit yourself to one particular kind of thinking, or thinking has a matter of reason, you could be missing out on a great opportunity to improve your consciousness about the truth, and of understanding the All from a more holistic perspective. Those who do not accept change, are lost and are meant to be defeated, by themselves. You need to defeat yourself, and you will understand things from all points of view, you cannot ever conform to one point of view, you shall always entertain an idea, even if you are against it, for from this you derive more reasoning by which your point may be further proved, or vice versa. Do not believe in the social dogmas, that say, men shall do this, and women shall do that, or any of that sort, never let yourself be compared to a collective, or never let the collective similarities be the reason behind the enslavement of your universal intelligence.

Always protect your individuality, always take care of the collective, but do not let this collective destroy or misguide you from your true path. Even if the collective was right, and human society was perfect, moral and spiritual, even then, the collective will be a pain to you. The path of the universal knowledge, is found within you only, and you should ask yourself all things that will lead to it, by knowing the nature of yourself, you know the nature of all things, and no further knowledge is needed, nothing will be surprising for those who know themselves, everything is seen a maze, in which different escapists must find the exit, but the exit is actually themselves. There is no difference when it comes to our universal dispositions. No matter how much you seek outside, you will never know anything if you don't penetrate into yourself with Love, or until you find that universal and unconditional love.

 This subtle love permeates all things, and in this devotion we may be able to expand our consciousness, and become one with All, for The All, is purely based upon love, love is everywhere, as is consciousness, to become the universal consciousness, you need to adhere to the universal love, and to the precepts that allow you to dispose your extra-spiritual layers of yourself to the truth and cosmic ideal made for you. When you entertain solely those things which you come to meet outside you, you only know the 1% of the All, you only know a relative part. It is not smart to try to understand a grain of the all, when you have the All just inside you. It is inefficient like nothing else that has stagnated the human being.

All intelligence, all knowledge, is nothing compared to love, love is in them all, but them all by themselves, and in division, cannot lead to love. Love and devotion is what ties all things together. You need to build yourself around a spiritual path that adheres to unconformist unrestrained love and curiosity, charity for all. The sole practicality is very simple, you need to, in every respect of your actionality, become universal, and adhere to the principles that lead to universal amalgamation, for which we shall provide the specific schemes later, that are practical for everyone that is open to it. But in general terms, it is actually the same for everyone, and everywhere in the universe and in every epoch, this truth has existed, the greatest truth is love, love is above all things, love defeats death, and it defeats ignorance.

Apparently, this is not true, but if you think clearly about this, you will find out that love is the truth, that is it is the only thing universal. Love is the only thing that brings about the invisible, the incredible, and the inconceivable. Everything else is revealed under the condition that you are within its same dimension, but love opens to you all dimensions, all points of views, it lets you get deeper into the empathic essence of the other. Love will never betray, but knowledge will, knowledge will not provide love, but love will provide knowledge. Knowledge is power, but without love, no knowledge will become available beyond the barriers of the crude, and thus, the universal consolidation is impossible.

This is extremely important, you must use the power of your mind to love, you must open your mind to new points of view, you must never let dogma enslave you. You must focus on love with ideation, with the knowledge that everything is it, and that the All is within you, and thereafter, what before was unclear will become clear, what before was hidden will not be revealed, and the key of keys, the one that unlocks all doors will be your present, literally and figuratively. As long as what you do in life, no matter what it is, lacks empathy and love, then you will never know the full extent of all elements.

Start by getting out of your comfort zone, and accepting that the path to cosmic knowledge is within you, that you have within yourself an antenna to the Source. Start by listening to what is not being spoken, to see what is not visible, to touch what is not palpable, to smell what is not in the air, and to taste what cannot be eaten, and to think about all these things with love. Read what is not written. You have to perceive all things as yourself. Wherever you look, you must know that you are one with that thing, you must change your outlook, you must feel universal, you must not overthink, but act as the All itself, and all fears will leave you, all secrets will be revealed. You must not let the dogmas of the distorters of the truth get to you, you must only believe in nature and the

All, in the truth itself, and not in the relative truths that seek to undermine your universal knowledge. Universal knowledge is already inside us, in the infinite power of our spirit, that is a fragment of the All itself, look out the outside world as it being inside you, and look inside you as having the outside already in all its forms inside you.

The greatest secrets, knowledge, prophecies, and more, are found within you. All wisdom is within you. All solutions are within you. All intelligence is already within you. Universal, you must understand and apply this: it is impossible from external achievements or movements, it is only possible within yourself.

Everything you do, intellectuality, must follow this principle, if you fail to follow it, and follow the laws of the All, you will never attain such universal status and universal recognition. Do intellectual exercises that force us to see all things the same way, to find the relation among all things, to develop and understand the intricacies of the law of correspondence, in its subtle and apparent ways, forms and colors. See the invisible lines and links that connect all things, the plane is wonderful, but even more wonderful are the connections that allow the plane to exit, and that make the inner the outer and outer the inner.

Change and evolution predisposes all things, all things will finally come together, all things are siblings to each other, and all fields of intellect can be applied to every and any of the others. Use them all, for all, and deploy all the other principles in relation to this channel of understanding and universal practice of intellect. Learn the All by the inner, and the inner by the All.

Let your perception of reality be both lineally radial and radially linear, so that no factors may be left out, and all patterns may be found. Be ready to be blind after seeing the light of the truth, which is found within the universal knowledge, the complexity of this truth of universality, and the many patterns that are hidden, is transcended through simplicity and love, without these, you will never be able to transcend all patterns, you may become an erudite, but your consciousness will not be open to all patterns in predisposition, but in the degree to which you can realize through the analytical transcendence of the crude factors, but when you become subtle, you start to see everything as one, and no links of such will surprise, the generality of all things, and their specifics will become clear.

14. The Applicative Means to Achieve Ultimation

How many have you proposed yourself to do something, and yet you didn't do anything? How many times have you told yourself that you were going to stop doing something, yet could not? This is because the mind of the average person is weak, and their will is weak, they cannot fight against their desires, their instincts control them, and they do not practice what they preach or what they think is right. The problem of this world is mainly that people confuse the theory with the practice. They daydream and imagine, dream about so many things, they may think they are materialists, or pessimistic, yet the truth is that they were too idealistic or optimistic, or they were so from an illogical and limiting point of view. The problem is not that you have high expectations, but that you don't know how to direct them.

 Ultimately, the power of will and wisdom is within you. It is up to you to do what is right, beyond any kind of social norms or imposed customs. The goal is waiting for you, the goal will not come to you but you must run to the goal, just like you don't defeat the enemy by escaping from it, but by confronting it. If you are not practical when it comes to intellect, then intellect will not be able to manifest in the right manner within you. Do not confuse being practical with being limited. The true practicality is the unlimited spiritual practicality, that allows the human being to utilize the full extent of his power and all his spiritual potential. The potential is always within your election.

You must choose and be determined towards the goal. You must be disciplined, and take into account all these points I have spoken, and you must have an unwavering faith that you will do what is right, that you will start the process. Do not see the goal as the process, but the process as the goal. If you only think about the goal, but do not have the will or discipline to see the good experience in it, you will never apply yourself to it. If you solely focus on the goal, then you will become a slave to laziness and lethargy. The goal comes to you naturally when you enjoy the process, and your goal is not within the motivation of the goal, but the fascination of the process. For the motivation is there, but if you lack the fascination then you will not continue it till the end. For this you have to take into account your interests, and mix your practicality or wisdom with your interests, and change these interests as you change these goals.

Take advantage of the fact that you do not have to become a slave to any field as it is the case with the spouse, the intellectual spouse is a relative one, a universal one, as Creation itself, and so, it can change in accordance to interest, the opportunities for you to progress on the path of intellect are infinite if you don't think that the doors are going to close for you, you must always think that the doors will always open, and that there are trillions and more doors that will open. Intellect is not solely what we learn, but how to apply what we have learned, in regards to the most important of knowledge. So many intellectuals are false, are failures, because they solely work from the perspective of a theoretician, are lazy, and refrain from practicality.

This is a huge mistake, because wisdom cannot be proved if not through the practical, wisdom is not within words but within actions, is not within books but within trees, not within artifacts or technology but within nature. That's why nature and wisdom are the same thing, and the same is true for the field of intellectuality. To be practical in regards to intellect, is to be a physician that heals the disease in true stance, and doesn't prolong the disease to benefit from the sickness, this is the case for the intellectual leaders too. All intellectuality is meaningless if it cannot be proved in front of our eyes.

The problem is that there is too much theory and very little practice, too much laziness and no work, too much conformism and not hunger, too much self-imposed limitations, and not enough expansion of consciousness. All these things lead to the impractical intellectualism of the current days that seek to enslave the human being. You have to operate in the total opposite of all these things. You have to be positive in all virtues. If something seems too relative or social, then try to find its points of inflection in the social sphere, try to bring to practicality, it is simply that you are limiting yourself, do not limit yourself ever, always seek what is best for humanity, and practicality and wisdom will always come to life.

 Obviate the common people, for they are mostly ignorant, and they will do whatever it is told to them, you have to find your own path, you have to be the friend of nature, of the truth, that is your greatest friend as Newton would say. Focus on the true only, the true becomes wisdom, and the stagnation from the truth is derived from lack of will.

You have to improve your wisdom and your will, by building character, faith, hope, and reflecting about your own imperfections and experiences, only you can learn through your own understanding, wisdom can only be understood from internal experience, by speaking to yourself, and battling against yourself, but if you don't engage in these practices, and write down or think about the key points of what is truly worth, in life in general and in regards to intellect, then you will never be able to apply such wisdom to any of these fields. Do not judge others, until you think about these things, never think you know more than the other, for you can always learn from the other, you can learn more from a fool than from a priest, and more from a child than from a common adult.

For what is the point of being an adult, or purporting to be wise, if by your actions you negate your words. This is the same for the intellectual field. Apply these points, and take into account that there will always be new secrets to intelligence, for intelligence is universal and is always evolving. What tomorrow makes you intelligent, yesterday used to make you a fool, and henceforth. Apply these laws of wisdom whatever it is that happens, new doors will be opening to you, it is your decision to see them or not, to accept them, or to ignore them. Or the secrets, and this is the true secret, are actually in front of you, even the king of fools can get the truth by being sincere, and sticking to their true self, to their righteous self that satisfies God, and brings his grace, that is the true blessing.

 First, seek the moral, the natural and spiritual wisdom and will, and then all intelligence will be given to you, and all the intelligence in the world will become available to you, and as Tesla would say, you would advance more in 10 years than you did in the previous 1000. Many are called but very few respond. Do not see disadvantages all around you, but only advantages. The truth is simple, deception is complex. Because the truth is simple, you do not need intelligence, wisdom is within simplicity, and so is spirituality. This path of the intellect is more practical, and actually, easier to follow. While the theory and over-complexification of things will only lead towards suffering, accept the truth, that is what your spirit wants, that is what will lead you to the application that is best for you. Let your own ego die, for it only wants to be fed deceptions, and the false expectations of society, that will never be the truth.

The hardest of all missions is the simple one, the simple acceptance that the whole structure and vibration of society must change, and if it does not change, then society will never develop its utter intellectual potential. You will always be an "almost", an "it could have been more but it was denied by the will and neglect of the people". You may think this is false, but this is all due to your ego. Let your ego go, let your false self go, let your spirit be, let your true self be. The best practicality starts by your thoughts, control your thoughts through meditation, through self-control. Guide your beliefs through logic, never limit yourself, let reason be open towards all points of view, towards the meta-sphere. Combine all these into the physical, mental and spiritual world, and all that will occur. Just as you are reading this book without actually thinking about it, so engage in these secrets without thinking much, just do it, just experiment it, so that you truly understand it and see the progress.

Do not speak, act. The moment is now. Do whatever is in your hands so that you can also help society and those in need. Be like God himself, and you will ultimately become, and gain his intelligence, believe yourself in this manner and the practical will occur. Once again, look at the animals, they do not speak, yet through their actions they are intellectual in a practical manner. Then, how much more could you not be if you were intellectual in this same degree and without saying a word, but accepting the truth, applying it and learning the secrets in this silence of your will. When you silence your ego, your mind, then the truth will arise. Be a practical intellectual, do not overthink, think properly.

Do everything in moderation. Do not even take these secrets if you don't want at first, only try to experiment and see if they are true, try to apply them and tell everyone, if they work for you, apply them, or if you had already executed them unconsciously about them, then do not worry about them. Just know that these are drawn from logic, if you do not follow them, and focus on false expectations, then the goal will never come to you, you will always spend your days daydreaming and waiting for something to happen. Opportunities for improvement do not come to you, you must go to them, and just like that, do them, think through your actions, be your actions be your words, and you will get all this right.

Part 3: The Societal Ends of Intelligence

15. The Societal Ends of Natural Affinity

What is the ultimate point of natural affinity, what is natural for human society. The natural way is to act, just like an animal would do, in a human intellectual manner. Instead of trying to act like a human, the ultimate end of natural affinity is to become a beast, become a beast so that you may be able to become the best human you can possibly become. Humanity, and its society itself is like a remembrance of human society society, it is similar to the way the human mind or the human body organizes itself, but only that society is the body of the collective, its many humans are the cells, and all these human must, through their social life, accustom and become interested in the great truth of natural affinity.

Every action of yours must be directed towards the natural path, when you socialize and interact with others, you shall use such natural affinity for the common good, and not for your selfish self-interests. After all, the learning of nature is an external one, by learning about nature you are learning about something that is somehow external to you, especially when it is intellectual, when it is spiritual, it is nature that is inside, for we are not only inhabiting nature but nature inhabits us. Every action unto others, because it is external, must come under the compromise of wisdom and knowledge, it cannot ignore these facts, if we ignore this great truth, we ignore the greater aspect of human life, and that of morality. Natural when done externally, must be moral.

Nature is not independent, but itself is the interdependence of all things. The human way of life comes under the rule of nature. When you speak to someone else, when you help someone else, when everything you do unto others, you are doing to yourself. This is undeniable.

When you see the herbs close to each other in the fields of grass, you don't see them fighting each other, yet there they are, and they work exactly as they do, but when you see human beings, who are animate, and who have will, they fight each other, and all nature is destroyed. There is no greater natural intelligence than that of self controlling our will and directing it to the right ends. Our inherent path is the natural one. It is extremely hard for the normal person to discover this by themselves, they need to reflect upon their life a lot, and commit lots of mistakes before they are able to learn the truth in such manners.

If the herbs lack intelligence, yet their natural intelligence among themselves is superior to you, how much more would you be able to do when it comes to the collective impact. If herbs were to be animate and have will, and if they maintained this level of perfection, they would be God, but there are no grasses but human beings, and human beings are destroyed through their intelligence. Their intelligence destroys their natural path. The natural societal path is one that is more lacking in will than it has of it.

To help somebody does not need much thinking, when you help someone naturally, you don't think much about it, but when you are going to hurt someone, you think much about it, you have to plan for things and you have adrenaline rushing through you. In this way, it is clear that will incline human beings towards decline, but when human beings do what they ought to do, in a natural manner and without any sort of will, they do what is right and the world is a better place. The perfect intelligence when it is outwardly directed towards society, is one that leads nature towards nature, and humanity towards humanity. Meaning, that humanity may combine their will, or they perfect subtle control over the same, with intellect, and that when these two forces are combined, human capacities and inherent abilities, which are mostly the cause of their own imperfection, may be transmuted so they become the source of their perfection.

Natural intellect has to be a combination of intellect and lack of the same, of will and lack of the same, meaning, more is not always more but less, and less is actually more, you have to find your point of moderation, and such must be case of most of society, society shall be ruled by these rules of nature such as those of balance, adaptation, self-control, consciousness, etc. If human beings do not adapt to such laws, they will be lost, and they will be maintaining this wrong philosophy of life, where nothing is natural, and because you, through your own actions, do inherently wrong unto others, all these things you have done will come back to you. If it is like this, if it is to not meet the rules that are best for yourself and for all, and would be better for you to do nothing, and to not try to find natural intelligence. Because your intelligence and your nature are individual, so are the ways in which you can help others, you can become perfect, but this perfection doesn't need to be universal, you can help nature your own way, this intelligence can be individual, because universality is in pluralism, you do not need to do what is of of others, for we are all individuals.

The best intelligence we can provide is our individual one. Perfection is found when you help others find their true nature. Use this intelligence, to copy nature, and to apply the ways of nature to humanity. There is no better way to help humanity, than through the love of nature, and the intelligence of nature is better than all human teachers combined, and the intelligence of nature is superior and heals better than that of all human doctors in the world.

Nature will not betray you, nature will not lie to you, nature will not hurt you, this is impossible, nature will only do what is right to you according to your will. There is nothing better for the upliftment of humanity than to teach the ways of nature. For in nature is perfection, but in human will there is only imperfection and evil. When we are in nature, when we learn from nature, we don't need anything else, nature makes us possess the ultimate liberty and the ultimate independence.

No one can feed humanity, no one provides more food, more abundance, than nature, nature is eternal feeder, all these leaders you see around, are all imperfect, and they will not lead you anywhere, the way of truth, is the way of nature. Nature is the only teacher, the only healer, the only provider, nature gives you more than you ever wanted, even when you ignore her. If you study nature, if you apply yourself to it, you can help humanity better than everyone has, and you will surely attain perfection. Perfection is only possible when we look into nature, when we look into the common ways of God.

Humanity will heal when they turn to nature, and every law of society shall be based upon nature law, for it is the true law, the law of peace, the law of all that which humanity needs. In this law there is humanity's true path, for it is not subjective or based upon opinion, it is based upon the inherent perfection of nature. Every building, every gadget, every invention and technology of humanity, shall be made just as an extension of nature, as the builder of all that is right. When humanity becomes the epitome of nature, through her intelligence, and ability to manipulate the same, she will become and know perfection.

But when humanity only uses her intelligence and her capacity for nature only in selfish ways, she will remain imperfect and without clear signs of evolution. Nature being the only source of this same evolution. The intelligence of God, that displays in nature, wants the best for us, but doesn't want the best for ourselves, or we look for the best for us in places where it is only delusion and pain, and not the right thing to do. We are deluding ourselves into the acids of the aberrant and artificial.

All this intelligence of nature we abusing, and doing for what is wrong to hurt others, and to all kinds of things that are against morality and spirituality, but you fail to remember that in these areas there is also nature, and that one part of nature fails, every other part of our nature fails, and society, is therefore, a fail. We shall under such predicaments always live in deception, we shall always be imperfect beings, and do just what is wrong. We ought to transmute the perfection of nature for our benefit, but humanity is so imperfect, that imperfection cannot escape her, and this imperfection, because of such being the outlooks, destroys everything around her, including the perfection of nature. From now on, you shall utilize and learn from nature in order to become perfect, and learn the truth.

You shall learn as an individual, as if nature was your sole master, and you must obviate the collective ignorance, the common person is usually an aberrant one, and who bases their existence on the aberrant intelligence that leads them towards destroying nature and leading humanity to the worse. Ignore all leaders, ignore all collectives, ignore all hate, all imperfection, all that which corrupts nature itself, and only pay attention to her, and in her you will discover the truth and discover that when we are in silence, when we help in silence, when we recognise in silence, we we speak the truth in silence, when don't try to impress the other, we will still be recognized by nature, and she will give all that she has in the best way for us.

16. The Societal Ends of Sexual Transmutation

A great deal of the social interactions of human beings; of that socialization process, is based upon the fact that it deals with sexuality. Since young, our mothers feed us, and take care of us, and in that process there is pretty strong sexual remembrance, which may not be direct, but rather indirect, the same occurs in the phase between infancy and adulthood, in which socialization is greatly influenced by this sexual development of this stage of life. Now, when there is no restraint to this process, humanity goes into a negative loophole. Violations and aberrations start, and violence comes to life.

This is greatly due, in fact, to the fact that the relationship of these people to sexuality has been negative, repressed, and barely if not transmuted at all. The societal transmutation of such energy shall be a creative process, through creativity, energy, strength of will, and so many other qualities like this, human beings are able to cooperate better, without any restraint, with all transparency. When human beings over-indulge in such sexual activities, they start to feel a subtle shame, and subtle change in their perception that turns them to act in certain ways, and their true self or positive side is blocked. Where they would otherwise see an opportunity to help, to maximize the progress of humanity, they see only sexual cultivation, where they could learn and teach, improve society and themselves, they see more of this same force.

Sexual unrestrained force leads to a blindness of the external mission, of that it is that we came to this world to do, and that in this way we shall help the others. When we perceive only through the sexual lens, we only perceive our own pleasure, and we neglect the well-being of the other, this is complete blindness over the moral truth of human conduct. What before was mere pleasure-hunting, now becomes serious immorality. Because sexuality is the gateway between morality and immorality, between the search of truth or the delusion with deception.

Sexuality is inherently egoistical when not restrained and expanded like a virus over the whole society. Sexuality only satisfies the lower pleasures, and the intellect is damaged, the human being does not seek discovery, the human being does not want to create for others, as they would for themselves, the human being, cannot spark that curiosity to know more and acquire more wisdom. All human endeavors, and their intellect in attachment, are driven into waste and obstructed. When you only see the wrong side of something, the truth of the positive side shall not become apparent, and it will be hard for you to find it.

We should not only transmute our own energy, but should help others transform theirs, in this process they will be led towards God, and immorality will seek from planet Earth. In school, in the mentoring process, sexual energy shall be seen as a key factor for it, sexual energy, ought to be like the branches of a tree when it comes to the pedagogical process, the person that knows the power of the various manifestations of this energy shall teach those who don't. The edifices shall be built in such a way that they create a natural imagery, and that, thanks to other factors we shall herein list, this process may become more simple. If there is a need to fight, this fight shall not be external, for this is what happens when sexual energy is not transmuted, that we confuse our own struggles with any relation we have to society, society itself would gain more if each person picked up a fight with themselves, and if, instead of trying to involve others in this energy, this energy was culminated into themselves.

Sexual energy is related to our willpower, and to what degree we are violent to others, or to what degree we need others, instead of needing of and for ourselves. The person that can control this energy, will not be led into senseless fight and division towards others in human society, he will be contemptuous to judge himself, and judge not the other, in this way, society would flow in a judgementless state, and people would express themselves in their positive sides. But because the positive is unfairly criticized, the negative side manifests. Our struggle with our own sexual intellect, the peace within us and to others, and intellect all the same.

If our intellect is solely wasted on others, and in pleasing ourselves and the others, we harm the others in this pleasure as much as ourselves. Self-improvement, in its collective form, is superior to mere collective call for help, and support, that may actually turn very individualistic, for all is internal, and the external without the internal is meaningless. Intellectuality can only help others, if we can help ourselves with it, and sexuality can only help others, if we can help ourselves with it, and not less is the relation of these two. If we don't transmute our own sexual energy, we cannot expect to help others in this same process.

The creative power shall be used in forward and reverse. The construction of your mind shall be used to create gates of psycho-physical order, through which sexual energy may be transformed for the improvement or boost of all these intellectual capacities, or factors that lead to the same. The serpentine rising of your kundalini force, that is actually sexual energy, is to be used to, and its same force and order, help others, and construct technologies that may help others. If this force is the force of God, of masculine and feminine within, then its externalization will bring nature to human society, and we may be able to duplicate and imitate nature as it shall be, to its optimal form, in such a way that the grade of its sophistication, does not invalidate the alienation of the same with natural order.

But if this intellect is not propelled or boosted by this sexual force, then all its externalization will be aberrant and it will always lead us not very far, but into straight line, a straight line does not go very far, further can take you the spiral of this supreme force, for it takes you inward, towards itself. The sexual transmutation of sexual order, that is intellectual and spiritual in character, must always be internal, it must be spiral, while the mere physical could actually be external, and like a straight line. To go out, you must go in, if not, you cannot properly transmute this sexual intellectual force. This help is a subtle one, one that is not that so evident as you would think, this help does not know of results, its results may not be clearly visible, or they may not be direct.

The true help done is the one that is not known, the one you do not know how it may end. Everyone can be artists in their own ways, this is the power of sexual energy, that even non apparently artistic tasks become artistic. Going back to the root tasks, manual tasks, will be the offshoot of this transmutation. These tasks are actually very intellectual, and they propel the intellectual potential of human beings.

These tasks help us focus on what is important, on what matters in life. Morality and intellectuality become one, and the human being finally redirects their intellect towards doing good to others, and not trying to undermine the potential of others. All animal relationships are based upon this sexual principle, they are part of this concept of union between two different parts to form a new one. This union is now becoming more psychic, the union is invisible, the union leads to things which we have never imagined existed.

When teams and collaboration takes the sexual root of human expression, the whole society walks towards God, when this sexual energy is elevated, nothing is impossible for humanity, and they may finally become Gods. If this fear, if this lower state of existence, based upon need and fears, bring the worst, if they are transmuted, they can also bring the best, for the extremes always have opposite poles. Humanity will not be aberrantly artificial, but righteously natural. We don't help others because we are scared, for one reason or the other, because we lack consciousness, because we see danger where it is not.

Because we see our need and not that of others. Through sexual energy transmutation, you have the opportunity to transform the need of others into power, and the dependence they have upon the material into independence. The same occurs on an intellectual level, and thereafter, you may not have to help them anymore. There is no greater help than teaching humanity how to truly be humans, by transmuting their sexual energies so that they may become Gods, when the ultimate point of this transmutation is achieved, even intellect in itself is meaningless, for God does not ask for this, but we can even live without it, the intellect rather becomes a state of flow, it becomes natural, and our whole existence becomes natural, and perfect.

The ultimate state of humanity is when we may establish a system wherein such energy is transmuted from young, that's when humanity will truly evolve, and they will achieve an intellectual advancement even beyond the level of genetics, for these latter will also change in accordance to this paradigm. What we want the most of the other, or the opposite, is actually what could help the most within ourselves, and that is the path humanity ought to take, and intellect will become the normalcy, and not the atypical formation of society.

17. The Societal Ends of Psychic Fascination

Different people may have different interests, they may change from culture to culture, etc. Whatever we could do in the individual mind, we can also operate on the collective consciousness. Society is to be based taking into account the fascination of each individual, and how individuals who present the same fascination can work together. This is key, not only for the intellectual aspect, but also for the overall state of human society and for the peace and harmony that is needed so that progress can exist. When people share the same interests, things go smoothly, and the chemistry is better when working together, and everyone evolves together faster.

Sadly, these differences or similarities are not taken into account, and people end up interacting that should have not interacted in the first place, because their personalities are the total opposite. This is the cause of so many conflicts, wars and misunderstandings, and therefore, of human progress in regards to the intellect. When all these things exist, when there is constant conflict, society cannot progress, and there is no place for the creative mind, or for intellect to develop. Rather, our intellect and fascination will always be crude and directed towards war. Humanity will only be thinking about new weapons that can more easily kill the other, of better products relating to mundane pleasure, etc.

That's why the main ending point of fascination in society is that it should lead towards a better future harmony and flow in society. When humanity is in such a state of flow, things go smoothly, just like the river flows or the body does its many functions, but when fascination and its intellectual byproduct are not taken into, society is diseased and built upon problems and problems that seem to have no end. The interests of society are fundamentally of two types, what is inherited given society and family, and secondly, what the leaders may do so that culture may change one way or the other. In this way, in societal understanding, the fascination of it is mostly predetermined, and very few ever have any control over their fascination, or the channels of predisposition of the same. Not only that, but many interests are built up from past lives, and the relation of the past thoughts with the current manifestations, given that certain kinds of people or reactivities are always going to be manifested in certain cultures.

For this, it is key that society must work together, and especially the leaders must become wise and knowledgeable of the great truth of fascination. It is key that these leaders can control themselves, so that they may be able to rule others, for those who cannot rule themselves, are victims of this fascination, especially the crude one, and they cannot control themselves, they do not have the requirements so that society can function correctly and in this equality of interest. Because of this sole reason society suffers much. We need leaders and rebels, who don't become the victim of this mere fascination that has been evoked upon us, we need to take care that this fascination does not become our enslaver, as it has been the case for so long. A crude fascination gives rise to materialist ideologies, a subtle fascination raises the idealistic and spiritual ones.

Materialist ideologies govern society, for erudites and political leaders of society and any other occult leaders, are also controlled by it. This then translates to the generality of society, because humans always act like sheep, and do what few leaders or influential people in society are doing. We need leaders that do not seek power, that do not seek to suppress society and its potential, that seek the truth no matter what, and recognize the power of fascination. At the end, whatever human beings may do, they will always be at the expense of this fascination, for it all is. In fact, the current society is enslaved by it because gadgets and instant gratification are a kind of crude fascination.

It has destroyed human intellect in countless ways. That's why we need to work together so that these artifacts of humanity do not become our own enemy, and they are used in the most moderate and efficient manner. They must be created so that the natural rhythms and cycles of the human body and neuronal, psychic system are not altered. The path of righteousness and reason is naturally a path that is to be taken by the route of proper fascination. The problem is that this route becomes so dangerous and harsh that we don't take it into account.

We are always living, as a society, in this vicious cycle that seems to have no end. One fascination leads to the other, and, as a result, we end up with the same power structures that seek to take control of the intellect and knowledge of the people. For this reason, the power structure is to be from the bottom to the top, and not merely from the point of view of intellect, but primordially from the point of view of morality. For more can the moral leader, than the solely intellectual leader, who does nothing but take advantage of the people through various means and machinations that set him apart from the apparently good leaders. It is best to be authentic and show our leaders just as they are, it would be more fructiferous for society if these moral and wise leaders created themselves the intellectual leaders, for at the end, the wise ones are those, that although not complexity or intellectuality developed, are able to be practical and pragmatic, thereby better helping society.

The control of fascination must be subtle, yet not complex, but simple, it is done from the simple to the complex, from the spontaneous to the planned. To go directly into planning is to not let things go, and one key aspect of fascination that it helps society is that it must flow, that it must not be stagnated in one point of society, or flow in society in such a way that it only helps a few. Just like the blood and lymph must not become obstructed, and reach all parts of the body providing oxygen therein, so must fascination be present in all parts of society in its right measure. For we will not ever reach true equality if this point of fascination, fascination and interest, and its utilization, are like the oxygen of society and the potentiality of people, when one part of society does not get enough, then the whole society will suffer and there will be inequality. In the pure material world, there may never be such a point of equality.

That was so dreamt, but we may reach it in the psychic world, and because of this, society will move towards one same goal in unison and in the formation of intellect, and camaraderie, there will also be the evolution of society as a whole. Evil and abuse are perpetuated in society because they are portrayed as something nice in the media, the idols are one of the key components by which people are inspired, either for bad or good, and education is too permeated by these people who impact society much. We are to take control of these forces, idols are to be proper and intellectuality is to be spiritual too, it must be subtle, and not guided by these false idols that are embedded in evil. We see how society is always going in circles, and never goes straight to what matters. People are fascinated by what does not matter,and the same is the case in the field of intellect.

People are fascinated by things that lead to nothing , that are not spiritual and do not direct us towards the truth. If we are fascinated by meaninglessness, so will our lives become. If we are fascinated by evil, so will our lives become. If society is not fascinated by intellectuality, and if their fascination is not transmuted towards such an end, human society will never become intellect at its maximum potential. There shall be certain knowledge in the general public that this force of fascination is truthful, and that it has the potential of changing human society.

If we obviate this force, we will suffer much, and we will not be able to achieve what we want. Morality and intellect go hand by hand, one without the other cannot exist. We cannot progress until we know the total extent of the influence of fascination upon our lives. There shall be a maximum study about this subject, about how it will impact us, about how it may be propagated in the most natural manner. Everything shall be tuned to the interest of the individual, for the collective, the individual, and for the individual, the collective.

We must see to answer the call of one and neglect the other, for then they will both go astray. It is better to please people according to what they like, then to create integral systems where individuality is destroyed, and that if there is any sort of collective order, this order must be compartmentalized under certain alignment that will bring harmony and flow to these groups of the social order. We shall not become overly serious, or overly fun, we shall have a moderation of both, but we shall know that fascination and excess of one and lack of the other can lead to all that is worth seeking or they will lead towards the greatest of pains. We cannot ever replace one fascination by the other, just as we cannot replace God. The third object or party is just like the first one, they will invariably lead towards imperfection.

The path is harsh but the reward is worth the suffering and effort.

When everyone enjoys what they are being taught, and when everyone develops their intellect by their interest, then intellect will become common order in society and we will reach our maximum potential.

18. The Societal Ends of Cognitive Isolation

Socialization is a key part of the human life, we agree to that, in fact, all animals socialize in one form or the other, to one degree or the other, all animals share the common denominator of coming together to survive and reproduce, the problem is that socialization is seen as only a human matter, when this is not the case, socialization takes into account other animals, the difference is that these animals do not possess all those qualities that make humans humans. To say that human beings are social animals, is a false statement, for all animals are social, human beings are not anymore social than any other animal on Earth, in fact, human beings, due to their will, have the capability more than any other being to not be social, and to refrain from contact with others belonging to their species. This is not necessarily bad, but another part of human life, so many people live in so many different ways, and this does not make them more intelligent.

We can agree, however, that the people that you go around with, are the people that are going to affect your intelligence too, and that sometimes, it would be better for a person to be alone, than to be beside such people. Many claim that socialization is an integrative part of the development of intelligence, even so, I would argue that this point of view is too ambiguous, and that socialization, as you can observe in society right now, hurts more than benefits the intellect of the human being. When the socialization process takes effect in masses, when people are led towards particular trends or forms of thinking, people do not act like individuals, but act solely like the ants or the wasps, but in a but way, but they follow the laws of nature, but human beings group, to instead, oppose the laws of nature and balance.

Therefore, in the masses, the process of socialization may lead towards the propagation of low intellect behaviors, that are copied in masses, due to the innate human tendency to imitate others, that comes from our infancy and mother and father. Socialization, therefore, is a tool that can either be used to help others through their intellect, or to completely subdue them. I would argue that first, people need to find themselves, people need to invert into themselves, and then they can go out and help others, but that having friends without meeting yourself is like having friends for nothing, for you cannot help them improve, without first improving yourself.

In the absence of any other other mean, in the absence of a proper socialization system, the best way to improve intellect is by being alone, and the best way, many people would do rather good than bad to the world, would be by isolating themselves, and accepting that they cannot live in human society. Many people, who undergo different mental disorders or divergent patterns, would have not committed any of these atrocious acts if they accepted this, and if they went and lived alone, they would, even further, better improve their intelligence by being, and so they would have helped society in a better way. The sole cause of many of these issues that permeate human society, is that people seem to have become attached or addicted, as we mentioned in the previous chapters, to all these things that propel them to be in these states of mind that are not favorable, neither for society nor for themselves.

If we look into what has affected human society, and also through the indirect effect of the same on human intellect, is that people have not found the manner through which they may not become attach and come into a constant overload of any information alone, creating a sequence of events that all lead towards the suppression of their creativity, intuition and so many other intellectual abilities. How can a person that is constantly attached to something, who is imperfect, and cannot live without something, be able to rule others if they cannot even rule themselves. For this reason, the perfection or pre-requisites, by which we may help others, is not only found within the interaction with the other itself, but to the empowerment of the invoker of the same through the moderate and efficiently rational negation of the same.

In other words, to isolate yourself, either from people or from the information derived from them, is not anti-social, is not necessarily that act of a bad person, of a renegade, but depending on society in which it occurs, it may be the preamble to better help through the strengthening of their intellect, or it may be the foundation of a revolution of an unrighteous society. Therefore, we can help as much in solitude and ignorance over society, as we can help by socializing, and the same is true in the intellectual form, for what intellect can a smart individual gain from a society of fools? How can a person who is guided by the aberration of the materialists, who is constantly seeking pleasure, who suffers from cognitive overload, help others?

This is an impossibility, at least in its most elevated form. For this reason, it is key that you do not see help in union, but also in the beneficent division. This may seem contradictory at first, but it actually is not.

Just like all other things, when we spend too much time together, we get tired, and then the fights start, that's why it is key, in society, either towards people or things, to get some free time, and instead, spend some time alone. Rest is needed, even when you don't sleep, you get tired and you start to function incorrectly, the same is true for your intellect in the social aspect, if you don't get some rest, if you don't think about society, and the way you interact with it, you will become habituated to the stupidity and aberration of society, and you will become a zombie, just as you become a zombie with the smartphones and drugs the create a neuronal and information overload in your brain. That's why those who get time alone, those who see friends where they are not, will be blessed, and they will find their peace.

On the other hand, those who are in constant need of the other, who need to socialize and be entertained and pleasured all the time, are actually the weakest, the most aberrant people, and they will not either develop their intellect or the sense of connection with the other in the most appropriate manner. This is especially useful in arenas such as prison, where people spend more time alone, wouldn't it be better if they went to nature, and you placed all the offenders of the same kind in one place, and you let them think and learn among themselves, and to make them socialize or receive information from any smart device or the TV. It is actually in these manners that the truth will be uncovered, if they suffer they will see the truth, and they will develop their moral intellect, otherwise, you are only, in a subtle way, focusing on the same problems that caused all these issues in the first place.

At school, some of the students discord the class, they cannot get alone the school itself, it would be then, better to isolate them, to place them all in one class, and to teach them through cognitive isolation, in other circumstances, for the manifestation of these symptoms, are the subtle defect in some other.

Students learn better with a personal mentor, why don't we let students develop learning by themselves, through nature, wouldn't they become more interested or get to utilize their interest for that particular area when they are by themselves. Isn't cognitive isolation a key through which many would now better control their instincts, and their sexuality, for through this, they can better control their will and their thoughts.

In this way, and in almost all areas of human society, the human being gets into itself, and becomes their best version, basically, who they truly are, while when they constantly seek the validation of others, it is their ego that takes control, and their intellect becomes as imperfect as their egos. When the spirit takes control, then in this cognitive isolation, human beings will, after now seeing each other for a very long time, get easily alone, and violence and all these things that permeate human society like viruses will cease. Sometimes, those who do not seem to love others, who seem to be antisocial, act in such ways because they don't love themselves, and they are angry at life, and have deep emotional blockages.

Through isolation, through one one one isolative measures, many of these issues can be easily solved, and we can better build society around the premises that it deserves, and intellect can be more easily developed. We can start by teaching children by isolation, solitude, and the many benefits it brings, from better creativity to better memory and all round intellect. It is especially the artificial that hurts human society, and creates this overload, it is especially the immoral and the materialistic, therefore, if there is any socialization, it must be under these basis, and it must not be predisposed towards the enslavement of the individual through the collective hypnosis and amalgamation of poor intellect.

Help others by telling the power of nature, and the law of Balance. Help too, yourself, so you can teach them this like a true master and from experience. Do not base your help around giving or trying, but around teaching and effort.

Politicians, people of power, etc, shall also account for the power of cognitive isolation, they should follow these measures themselves, so that they can truly help the rest of society.

19. The Societal Ends of Metacognizance Liability

If society wants to increase the level of intellectuality, and the degree to which this force can help uplift everyone in it, we must make sure that knowledge about intelligence has to be increased, and has to be studied in the whole society. The key factor that affects this secret in society is knowledge, whether derived from experimentation or from intuition, from the individual or from the conglomerate effort of a collective, knowledge about thinking, and thinking about thinking must be custom in society. Thinking about thinking is seldom a practice in human society, for most thinking that is done, requires itself to be external, requires the person to interact with an object beyond himself, so that he may be able to fulfill a task.

Sadly, this task, too, is a form of slavery, a means by which a few leaders can take advantage of the rest. When in solitude, when living in a more independent manner, that capacity to think by oneself becomes amplified, and human beings then assume, unconsciously and naturally, that the subject and the object must be the same, and that is within themselves. In this way, human beings will start to think more about thinking, and they will gain more comprehension about themselves, about what their duty is and about what they must do to win the satisfaction, not only of the other, but of God and themselves.

Therefore, before helping the other, or even so said, the primary help of society, shall be, that from a young age, all children are to be taught how think about their thinking, for in such manner they can better think by themselves, and by self-correction and self-reflection, they do not need the others to help them. This is even more important given the fact that human beings only increase their knowledge when they learn by their own experience, and by their own reflection, this is the way to perfection. If some other people come telling human beings that they must do this or that to become intelligent, it will not really bring a strong benefit.

Instead, the educational system shall be based upon experimentation and betterment of the individual. The individual is superior to everything else, the individual knows for certain what is best to him given his own experience, but if you teach without the practice and experience factor, then human beings will not develop a sense of individuality, and perfection cannot be found through the collective, but through individuality, for each person is different, and each person has a different set of ideas that work for them. You may argue that this is illogical, and that the human being cannot think by themselves, that they can only think if they are told this by someone else, but this is not true, everyone has the ability to think, but we have taught humanity wrong, and very few people have the capacity or consciousness to be able to think by themselves.

You may say that these aspects of the intellectual ability can be applied to everyone, this may be true in the effect, but not in the subjective application, for the mind and attractions and repulsions of each person is different, when a person is before any of these challenges, the challenges must be learned by the individual, and knowledge is the only thing that can be collectively given. Changing the whole culture of a society is a really hard task, and for this, we may need the help of nature, for nature is the expression of God beyond the human being, so there is no conflict between the human being, there is not man-made castigation but it all comes from Mother Earth, she knows what is best for humanity, if humanity doesn't want to accept her, then she will have to make them accept her. By this, we mean that the will of people to change towards perfection can only be a natural process, and one that is carried through their own will, we must live the collective and culture behind, we must leave behind this victim mentality that people have, and we must focus on each individual, and their will, if we try to make everyone learn and change towards a better way for their intellect and spirit, which may at time be the same thing, we will not get very far, for intelligence can only be gained when the individual learns.

That's why the relationship of a student with this teacher, shall be more akin to the relationship of a devotee with this guru, meaning; that there must be love involved in this match, there must be certain appreciation, of one for the other, and vice versa. The mentor must be, not only a mere intellectual, but a wise person, for there cannot be any teaching about perfection without wisdom included in it, for no one can reach perfection in their intellect, that has not become wise in the same, that has not loved the use and application of the same. Without love, without experience, there is no room for self-improvement, everything becomes robotic, and will, but programming is part of human growth.

If we must be teach people the knowledge about how to improve their intellect, it has to be based upon their own will, and it must not have any agenda beyond the same, the leaders and mentors, teachers, investigators, scientists, and whatever else, must not base their teaching upon their own benefit, but they must work solely for the benefit of society, and even more so, for the benefit of each person, and that they must never see society as a mass of people over which they can take advantage. The work must be divided into three categories: the physical, the psychic or intellectual, and the spiritual. Each of these areas must be given their particular importance and resources, there must be a clear method by which each of these points is achieved, without it compromising the maintenance of certain acceptable and dignitary cultural norms and customs, and without obliging the individual, let the work be subtle, and rather than forcing, the individual shall be naturally persuaded, and there is no better way to persuade than through the example of the perfection of the other, when a mentor, leader or idol, researches this level of perfection, than the other will want to obtain such level of perfection, there are already many examples, but they are ignored, now it is good time to revise them and make them known to the public.

For everyone to become a genius, we must study and understand geniuses, and not simply state that this or that is genius. Genius is a relative word, and by this same relativity there are means by which this knowledge can be used in society. It is especially effective in societies that are lacking in certain aspects, these aspects or drawbacks of the social norms can be greatly fixed if all these points are addressed.

People who suffer certain intellectual lagging, must be equally helped, this knowledge is of vital importance to them, and even more vital to them is the spiritual knowledge, all points of this divulgation of metacognitive knowledge must be spiritual, or otherwise society will not reach these levels of intellect desired. At home, these habits must be fomented, and the importance of habits must be taught. From a young age, people shall be taught to think by themselves, and align themselves with nature.

Habits, such as reading, writing, thinking, creativity, etc, must be established since a young age, and the educational centers shall be more pragmatic, objective and practical, they must not provide solely one part of the story, but account for all points of view, and they must not only provide knowledge, but there must be exercises, competitions and sports created solely for the upliftment of intellect, and the knowledge about the same. Sports like chess, and other creative means must be found so that society sees intellect as simply another sport, as a form of beauty, of art, by which they can gain recognition from society. It is only a manner of perception.

If the perception is materialistic and physical, then this will be society, and the leaders and followers will all behave like this, but if society is embedded with a more intellectual culture, then the same thirst for intellect and intellectualism will be occurring in society. It is only a matter of leaders, gears, time and habit. If these factors are met, then society will direct their efforts more towards intellectuality, and people will base their status, although in a materialistic form, more on intelligence, then, the highest forms of intellect, will automatically become spiritual, and therefore, will spirituality become the basis of society.

Not only does intellect lead to intellectuality, but spirituality towards intellect, one fulfills the means and ends of the other, in its transmutation, application and satisfaction for the human being.

It is like the spiral raising through the human body spine, and that is guided by these three forces, human beings are the combination of these three parts, of three ways towards truth, and of three ethical principles, all these lead to the progress of the whole humanity, when progress is lacking, then you cannot expect much from human society.

How different would society become, if they tried, at least, to follow these easy principles, and society must also base all their constructions and dispositions towards these factors, they must work towards perfection, and they must understand that perfection is never found within immorality, that as long as there is such immoral order, human beings will not raise very far, they will stay behind, and they will never be themselves, but the perfidious reminiscent of what they ought to be.

20. The Societal Ends of Universal Amalgamation

We live in a society, where everything is based off the idea of the self, even the so-called collectivist society, indulge in such principles by following the me-against-them principle, adhering to nationalism, and the group, then, is not universal, and becomes an individual in itself, that ruled by a very strict group of people, it becomes the spirit of a few, and thus, it is not really a collectivist society.

The true collectivist society is the universal and spiritual one, one that adheres to empathic and devotional principles that are beyond any barrier and sentimentalism of the dogmatic. Lack of spirituality in itself leads to lack of universality, for these people are afraid of the other, because they don't feel strong by not following the path their subconscious knows they ought to be taking, they instead, follow a false path as portrayed by their ego. In this state, society is always in a survival mode, and the opportunities for help are ignored, and the dangers are amplified, and when we amplify the dangers, we amplify the fear.

This is why we see, in the mass media, that all news are events of negative connotation, for that way fear is impressed upon the people, and the people cannot comprehend things from a universal and empowered perspectives, but only pay attention to this danger, that is so popular and supposed to cause great damage, even to the point of death. Even lack of universality leads to lack of spirituality, many do not discover the truth, because they don't accept doctrines beyond their self-grown imposed beliefs they obtained since childhood. They seem to be incapable of loving all things, or at least, to see the truth where it actually is, and thus, they cannot follow a true spirit, only being led by false premises that lead them nowhere. The question of universal intelligence, and universal support for the rest of society is one and the same.

 By discovering how we can help the other, from an authentic and loving perspective, we also discover the universe, we see in everything a utility, and thus, we see its why. When we are selfish, we only see our perspective of utility, and thus, only one form of causal correspondence is revealed unto us, but when we see things as they really are, as a universal pattern that is connected, and can serve all, then, and only then, can we realize the true intelligence in all things.

Wherever and whenever we see use in something, we must love that something, and we must see a pattern, and thus, a form of intelligence in that something. The forms of intelligence are countless as the constellations. As the forms of the grains of sand. As the shapes of water. Understand that what we know of this ocean of knowledge is nothing compared to the great knowledge that is out there. This is why, as a society, we need to learn to love, and help all, for in this way we can appreciate the All, and we can appreciate the Creator. We must go back to when we were children, and when we asked the whys of all things, in this why, there are also the ways in which we can help the other, and above all else, ourselves.

Society shall be taught to appreciate nature, animals, minerals, and the world around them more, for human beings are to encrusted unto themselves, in this manner, they cannot learn much, they can only see what their ego wants, and the occult defects and ephemeral nature of these desires, which they ignore. For everything in nature except ourselves has the answer to all our problems. We need to be more humble, and appreciate the perfection of nature, for in their silence we may find the answer to our wobbles. Understand that if we don't love anything at all, we don't love everything, for what we do to one, for we cannot ignore what we do to the others, and if you are not able to do this, you have to accept that you are defective being, and need to learn and grow of your own drawbacks.

The more we identify with all things, the more easily we may find the solution to our problems, for the greatest the factors the greatest the hidden relationships. When we see a person suffering, we must not just focus on their sole suffering, we must focus on the subtle cause of their suffering, we must find even the most little of all things that would help this suffering person. You may think that you are not them, but in reality you and them are one, and if you do this to them, the same will be done to you, and that is why, we may appear different apparently, but at the end we are all one, and we all must go through the same problems and effects, under different faces but through the same soul. As bodies travel the soul, intelligence travels God. It simply is, and you cannot escape from it.

Do not ignore those who you hate, because of one reason or the other, do not ignore those with whom you may not have a good relationship, or those things which you may be disgusted about, for what could be a poison for some, could be a potion for others. If there are millions of relationships in the intelligence of the universe, there is even a deeper universe in the ways these can be applied to human society, and so, each person is different, there, within this help and evolution, the connection between two universes, that of the soul, and that of the cosmos. For one is nothing but the reflection of the other. One grain of salt, can provide more information about the universe than millions of them, and so, one person can provide more information about the deepness of God, than millions of people pulled together.

Where we see darkness, there might actually be the greatest of lights, and where we see light, there might actually be the worst of all darkness. Where you see construction, there might be a calamity, where you see destruction, birth might be given to a prophet. Even in the meaninglessness, there is meaning, death is just another phase of eternal life. The same is true for society, we can always help, we can always find new ways to help.

Every member of society is to be taught and trained according to these principles, in them a wise person is to discern the world of opportunities through which they may help the other through their intelligence. Not only that, for any kind of problem or suffering, there must be a scouting done, so that the best "soldiers" can be proposed to help someone who would benefit the most from their particular intelligence. This, without ignoring the fact that anyone can help anyone, can everyone have to offer themselves to help everyone.

When someone cannot help, some other person will be able to do so, and henceforth, when everyone or almost everyone is able, and sees no problem in helping, then society will flow by itself towards good, and intelligence will feed itself. But if society is built around a selfish doctrine, then everywhere and everyone will be limited, and all the possible connections and patterns of growth will not be seen. By helping and building an intelligence even of that which we feel so superior over, and we try to understand them and answer their questions, then society will be able to answer her own questions. Our wounds are the portal that leads to the change in the world, and that heals everyone else. Whenever we see a defect in ourselves, we will have the remedy for the defect of others, and we will equally possess a key by which we can awaken the consciousness of some other person.

No person is more ignorant about their defects than themselves, it is therefore, the task of the other, to, through their specific intellect, awaken those people. Everyone, through their particular kind of intelligence or set of the same, can build a wisdom by which they can change the other, and become their mentors, those who apparently are distinct, could secretly be the most connected,and those connected the most, could actually be the ones damaging each other the most. But the power of love is above all things, as long as there is love in all these methods, proposed, and thereafter developed, the true path and the intelligence will always be found. If there is devotion, then we don't have to worry about how things may end up in society. We must give each thing the value it deserves, and so it is for intelligence, we shall not spend much time one idle things, that will lead us to spiritual death, we shall give everything the measure of our time and intelligence it deserves, and if we focus in any of such things, it shall be for the right purpose, in ultimate stance.

We shall not equate the mere attachment, or emotional contentment between the mere egos of people, with the true values that matter in life, and the matter that values. We cannot all be distracted, and focusing on the meaninglessness that has now been created in society, and obviate all those that are being killed while all these things are happening. The suffering of one, is the suffering of all, and the suffering of all, ought to be the suffering of one.

The only difference is in recognizing once and for all that truth, and dispose all mediums for the universal understanding of reality, and the need we have to help all people, even if they are or seem people of lower standing, people who even are antipathy-makers, killers, robbers, they all are sequestered by a hidden intelligence, that can only be unlocked when we love all things, including hate itself. It is not that the evil people are too smart, but that the good people have deceived themselves into stupidity, and have allowed society to end in such a deplorable state.

21. The Societal Ends of Applicative Ultimation

We always value what good the others do for us, but we forget the others ourselves. We say that we will help this or that person, but in the end we don't help them. It has been said that teaching a man to fish is preferable to giving them fish. In the world of intellect, giving is meaningless, giving only leads towards the degradation of intellectuality. Technology that remembers cellphone numbers and so many other of these utilities are actually counter-productive for our intellectual capacities.

The best help we can provide is to teach people how to think, and open their minds, to themselves, or to a new world of ours that makes them discover themselves in their own way. We must provide what people need, without thinking much about it. The problem of humanity is that people think way too much about what may happen, about the consequences of their actions, or they think that they will die when death doesn't really exist. We must act and believe these words, for they are truthful. You must risk your own life to help the other, so that you learn the most yourself, and the others may learn too.

Don't judge people, but motivate them to improve and help them achieve their own path. If there is a path towards the strawberries, do not go by yourself and give them to them, but have them go themselves and teach them how to pick them. When a person suffers from lack of will or understanding, they are like water that must be frozen, so they get strong, and get a clear shape. You must not provide knowledge about the ultimate election directly, but you must create methods by which they can obtain the understanding themselves. You must create difficulties and challenges so that their will and discipline is improved.

You must always take into account their preferences and interests, their nature, so that you can align with their true self and with the macrocosmic nature. You must not open their eyes, for everything is already in front of them, if they had truly thought clearly about it, you simply have to open their will and their consciousness. Intellectual and lazy is a must combination, so you have to create a kind of warrior intellectual mentality, where the warrior struggles to find the truth, the truth seeker will not have the truth at his hand through these conformists and materialist ideologies, but he will have to be a spiritual warrior. A spiritual warrior is also a moral and natural warrior, so he must fight to defend nature, and to defend the dignity and well-being of people, and especially those who are suffering, those who are lacking, precisely, in intellect and basic education, for by helping and providing such factors to the others, they will receive more of the same themselves. They must be disciplined to use this intelligence towards benevolence, towards the betterment of humanity, and to not fall in the greed and lower-desires that seek to exploit them, to use it to hurt others.

Without moral discipline, and spiritual discipline, the ultimate degree of intelligence of the human being will never be developed, so it is key that they are trained to be punctual, diligent and accountable for their moral and spiritual actions. Do unto others what you would like clothes did to you, this is also true for intelligence. When you are not disciplined, and you lack, and courage, you are indirectly hurting others and doing what you wouldn't like them to do to you. Everyone would like to get loved and helped, and to improve in any area of life, including intellectuality, and as long as you don't help, you are not proving right to this wisdom. Help more and more, and the whole society will be benefitted, through the path and cult of action, by a paradigm and extro-introversive movement of good karma and benevolence, in this way, more people can enjoy the fruit of benevolence and the expansion of consciousness, by which their vibrations become subtle, and they are inherently and spiritually present in these intellectual tendencies.

You cannot retard this anymore, you must do unto others what you would like others did to you, taking time into account too, you must do it already, or you will never do it. Procrastination is simply derived from thinking about the past or future and neglecting the ever-going present, at which the truth is found. The present brings the present of concentration, emotion and idealization, it is the present that is all that matters, and in the present you must help the others elevate themselves intellectually, and apply any secrets or principles that you know. There are no secrets but everything is unveiled unto those who seek righteously. Divulge these secrets, for there is no better way to help the other than by unveiling that which is hidden to them, and that is hidden so that they may be maintained in this state of oppression.

There is no better way to help than by teaching wisdom, and wisdom is understood intellectuality by actionality, by practicality, by reflecting upon our own faults, and finding our own power. All intellectual barriers are broken within themselves, teaching about the science of introspection, and the discovery of our true capacities. In the games of wisdom and will, do not tell people to read this or that book, but to read themselves, do not tell them to understand nature, but to understand their own nature, do not tell them experiment with any chemical or substance, but to experiment with their own minds and body in moderate ways, do not tell them to become surrounded by smart people, tell them to be surrounded by God, that is within him, do not tell them to teach so that they will know better themselves, teach instead to teach themselves, to use their imagination and be humble on all these areas, so that ultimately the internal betterment becomes automatic by itself. This may all seem a contradiction, but they are all certain. Once society revolves around helping and giving, everything becomes easy, and all things find their place.

No more judgment, no more abuse, no more bullying, no more humiliation, but only helping the others. Practicality and people cannot develop themselves together when there are cumulative problems taking them over. Society cannot develop when there is an imbalance between theory and practice, and between the internal and the external, the good and the bad, and deception and truth. All things of true benefit in society find their way through practicality. We do not seek to neglect the teachings of theory, of developing intellect through them, but even more so, we can develop our intellect when we seek practicality and when we seek the moderate perfection.

Theories that neglect practicality are the definition of dogma, and only bring death and evolutive stagnation to humanity, the human will never be able to achieve evolution in terms of intellect because all thought is based upon false premises and dilemmas, that do not lead to the truth, but kill any hope for the average person. It is the difference between the dreamer and the doer. The dreamer only dreams what he wants, he only sees things in contemplation, he only thinks based upon what he thinks could happen, he is full of conditionals.

The doer is the one that actually seeks to prove if he is right, and does not base his work solely upon theory, especially if the same is driven by intellectuality and superficiality, by mere delusional dreaming without any corresponding intuition tied to it, or even without reason. He is constantly seeking the truth, and trying to prove, to find and fight till the end to find what the truth is, till it is in front of his eyes.

He does not speculate, but sees the clear truth, as it shows itself for everyone to see. It is extremely important that practice is not neglected, and that it may be combined with creative and open-minded creative and out-of-the-box thinking, or else we will always be slaves to monotony, to vague presuppositions that lead nowhere, except to death. Millions have died because of these theories and dreams, and ideal ways that were taken advantaged of by evil people. In the opposite direction, we can take advantage of the practical precepts and concepts, and we can build a new world that is based upon different stages of the process. A path of introspective practicality and extroversive theory.

Life will only bring forth more life, and more truth, yet the false theories will only bring death, falsehood and obscurity. Ideas shall not dominate the human being, they shall not be the weapon of a few evil that seek to dominate the rest, it is the rather the human that should have the greatest of all ideals, and that is, that the will of the human being, his wisdom, and his courage, can take him anywhere he may want, and are in itself the greatest ideal. In other words, there is no ideal except within our own spirit, within the inherent positive faculties and emotions of the human. If any theory, social or otherwise, lacks love, lacks courage, lacks spirituality, lacks dignity, lacks righteousness, lacks justice, lacks, in summary, anything that makes the human being human, then it should be denied and thrown upon rocks, and not people.

Do not throw rocks at people, but at the ideas that are the true cause of either the destruction or the empowerment of people. Bring to the world the ideas of will and wisdom, of consciousness and knowledge, and these shall be the only path. Effort, truth, and love, are the true path by which intellectuality, and in general society can finally evolve to become what it truly shall become.

Conclusion: Future of Intelligence and Spirituality

We have, hereby, come to the conclusion of this little work. The future of humanity will be bright only if human beings work together for the same goal, if they all work together for the same premises, and no one may be compromised because of them. Humanity needs knowledge, consciousness and wisdom, and they need to realize the power of these things, so that they can finally realize their full potential. Awakening is not present in seeing, for everyone can see what has been done, and what is still being done unrighteously everyday. The true awakening comes from understanding and from the opening of consciousness beyond the default nomenclatures. Until this does not occur, then humanity will not go very far.

Humanity needs knowledge, needs practicality within that same knowledge, and needs to be humble enough to accept the truth, even if from a relative perspective, in the voice of the other. In reality, all that humanity needs, is already present in every corner of the world, and in every person within these, and all these secrets are already being applied at this moment, but the ego does not let them see the truth, that the maximum potential of humanity is within generosity and humility, and not within greed and arrogance. With this simple emotional understanding, with this tolerance towards the other, we can see the truth they have to offer, even if it is not within our point of view. Nothing said is totally false or true in actuality, everything relative remains relative, and everything absolute remains so.

Therefore, to find the absolute we need to be tolerant, first, to all relativities, until this accumulation in a valuable order leads towards the absolute truth, that will benefit all of society. The mere difference is within opening your hearts, and accepting the truth, and in keeping this false mask in which our egos control us, and we neglect the truth found within the others have said. We need tolerance and empathy, and when we find these, all things concerning intellect will expand, and all these secrets will be revealed, and many more of the caliber.

The problem is that people do not really think, or they think is not part of their authentic will, but only a programming which they have been instilled to follow to keep them submissive. It is time to stop being submissive, and to confront the truth face to face, without any doubts and fear. Fear and dissatisfaction are the cause of all evil. As long as you remain this way, you will never open yourself to the universal truth, and that requires all those things which we have stated.

 If humanity wants to lift herself forward towards the truth, towards a universal betterment, you must change, you must be engaged in a constant struggle for the truth. If you don't accept this, then you will not go very far, and you will remain in this deplorable state, where all is done for the false, within and without, and when and where there are not morality, naturality and spirituality, the three keys that unlock the door of righteousness, and therefore, intelligence, for the human being. All the following practices support in your path of supreme intellectuality, and they are a must, at least at the base, if you want to truly attain that state of intellect that is able to break barriers:

Meditation

Meditation is the practice of thinking that you are infinite and allowing the mind to take the object of ideation. It is a positive ideation, not leaving the mind blank. You disconnect from the external world and the body, imagining it disappearing. Start maintaining this ideation and repeat the mantra **"Baba Nam Kevalam."** The ideation is that everything is God, everything is even, everything is infinite. Breathe in with "Baba Nam" and fill yourself with energy. Exhale with "Kevalam" and release all tensions and problems. This universal mantra helps in cleansing, health, and better discernment. Meditate twice a day for at least 20 minutes to develop the habit. Soon, you will raise your awareness and ultimately become one with the Supreme Consciousness, *Parama Purusha*.

Kiirtan

Kiirtan is the singing of a mantra out loud while the mind focuses on the Supreme Being. It instills a feeling of bliss and prepares the mind for meditation by engaging all motor and sensory organs towards the Supreme. The best time for kiirtan is just before meditation.

The mantra used is "Baba Nam Kevalam," meaning "my loved one is the only thing." The concept is to perceive the Supreme Consciousness in everything you experience. Kiirtan purifies the mind, accelerates the journey towards the Supreme, and provides mental clarity and relief from physical and psychic pain.

Sattvic Diet

A sattvic diet elevates consciousness and benefits the body, mind, and spirit. In yoga, there are three types of energy or gunas: sattva (pure), rajas (mutative), and tamas (static). These qualities are present in the foods we eat and the emotions and thoughts we have. A sattvic diet aligns with these yoga concepts, helping us reach the goal of becoming one with the Supreme.

Half Bath (Yoga Technique)

- Wash your hands.
- Wash in cold water (no soap required) from knees to feet and elbows to hands.
- Take a sip of water, hold your breath, and splash water into your open eyes at least 12 times.
- Splash water on your face, behind your ears, and on your neck.
- Take a glass of water, tilt your head back, and gently pour the water into each nostril 3 times, then blow or spit.
- Half baths should be taken every time you practice sadhana (meditation).

Fasting

Fasting has been practiced for health and spiritual reasons since the beginning of time. Fast every new and full moon, and 11 days after these. The moon significantly influences our psychic waves, similar to how it affects the tides. This influence is evident in menstruation cycles and the mental state of individuals, often referred to as "lunatics." Refer to a lunar calendar to know when to fast.

Nama and Niyama

Nama and Niyama are the moral codes of Yoga. They are essential for spiritual liberation and are divided into external and internal branches. The external branch deals with how an individual behaves towards the world and respects Creation. The internal branch deals with how a person thinks and the steps they follow to achieve spiritual aspirations.

Summary of Yama and Niyama

1. **External (Yama)**
   - Non-violence
   - Truthfulness
   - Non-stealing
   - Celibacy
   - Non-possessiveness
2. **Internal (Niyama)**
   - Purity
   - Contentment
   - Austerity
   - Self-study
   - Devotion to the Supreme

Conclusion

Incorporating these practices—meditation, kiirtan, a sattvic diet, half baths, fasting, and following the moral codes of Nama and Niyama—can lead to spiritual growth and a deeper connection with the Supreme Consciousness. These tools help purify the mind, body, and spirit, guiding you towards ultimate liberation.